THE

Fairy Bible

T0054595

THE Fairy Bible

THE DEFINITIVE GUIDE TO THE WORLD OF FAIRIES

TERESA MOOREY

UNION
SQUARE
& CO.

NEW YORK

Contents

Introduction

What are Fairies?

If this were an easy question to answer, fairies would not be the magic, elusive, ethereal beings that they are! Experience and belief in fairies varies from person to person and from culture to culture. These days many people do not believe in fairies, or at least feel foolish if they admit that they might—just might—consider that they exist.

It is easy to say that there is no such thing as the Fair Folk (another name for fairies) when you are in a city street at midday, driving your car, shopping, or talking on the telephone. It is a very different matter when you are out walking, miles from anywhere, and you find a bank carpeted with cowslips that seems to sing in the sunshine. It is also very different when you are alone on the moors and the mist is falling, or in a wood at midnight with the full moon above you. There your eyes may well be opened to the fairy power, and you will be in no doubt—no doubt at all, at least for a while—that these magical beings are real.

When we consider the enchantment of the natural world, we are drawing closer to a definition of fairies. It is best, however, to take a cool, dispassionate look at different beliefs about fairies in order to be as clear as possible about what they are and are not.

The logical, "scientific" approach is not to believe in fairies at all, stating that they are a figment of the imagination in the most trivial sense: at best amusing, at worst an ignorant or naive attempt to escape from reality (or, alternatively, a product of too much of the other sort of "spirit"). People who take that attitude do well to remember

that science and logic have not explained everything, and believing that they can and will (note the word "believing") is actually a belief stance in itself. To *believe* that our current perspectives on the Universe are some kind of culmination—that we have basically "got it right" and that all we have to do now is fill in a few blank spaces in order to complete our picture of existence—is arrogant and conceited. It closes our eyes; and it can tempt the fairies to play their tricks on us.

Some people take a positive attitude to the imagination, and visualize fairies as meaningful symbols that arise from the unconscious mind. From this perspective, fairies are important and call for reflection, although they are no more "real" than last night's dream. (Dreams, of course, beg a whole set of questions themselves, but let us leave them to one side.)

SPIRITS, ANGELS, OR DEVILS?

Fairies may also be regarded as the spirits of the dead, or the ancestors, returning with gifts of wisdom or warning. Many tales recount how people were taken bodily into Fairyland, riding with the Fairy Host in and out of hollow hills. Celtic people believed that the Land of the Fairies was also the domain of the dead. Fairies have been defined simply as one type of spirit of the dead—those that remain bound to the earth and that have not yet moved on to their eternal abode, wherever that may be.

Possibly fairies are angels, from the lowly sections of the angelic ranks, here to watch, guide, and bless us. Less pleasant to contemplate, they may be devils, trying to lead us astray. Fairies may be neither angel nor devil, however, but a sort of inferior spirit that got "caught" on the earth plane and never made it to Paradise. They may even be aliens that have landed from UFOs. Less fancifully, they might be a pygmy-type creature or a strange animal or bird, glimpsed only rarely (similar to the Yeti).

FAIRIES' TRUE IDENTITY

Proper fairies (with the exception of angels) are none of these things. They are beings who inhabit the Otherworld— a dimension of existence close to our own, which overlaps with ours from time to time and from place to place. For some people, the Otherworld, and its fairy denizens, is ever-present. Fairies are nature spirits, who tend growing things; they are the elemental entities of Air, Fire, Water, and Earth; they are the ancient goddesses and gods. Yes, they may also be angels—spirit messengers bearing wisdom—and they can be creatures of mischief. Many are mighty and awesome; some are terrifying; plenty are helpful and playful; but all are fascinating.

Fairies demand (and deserve) respect. Learn their ways in order to experience the best of them.

The Case of the Cottingley Fairies

There are many traditional accounts of meetings with the Fair Folk, as described in this Introduction. However, the case of the Cottingley fairies is comparatively recent, and more controversial.

In 1917, Elsie Wright and her cousin Frances Griffiths claimed to have had encounters with fairies at their home in Cottingley, in the English county of Yorkshire. In 1920, the writer Sir Arthur Conan Doyle published an article in the *Strand* magazine concerning the photographs of fairies taken by the two girls. Many people, including some respected thinkers, believed in nature spirits; but, needless to say, there was scornful criticism from some sceptics.

No one was able to prove anything conclusively until the cousins—by this time old ladies—owned up to having faked four of the five photographs; and many people believe the other photo was also a fake. Late in life, Elsie stated that she never really believed in fairies. Frances, however, was a very efficient matron in a boys' school and had a reputation for total honesty; after she died, her daughter described her as a woman who could never tell a lie.

A QUESTION OF CREDIBILITY

Stories of encounters with supernatural beings frequently present problems. In the first place, people often choose not to believe what they see, and would rather assume they have imagined it all than face the fact that their view of

"reality" could be deeply flawed. Some may be tempted into faking proof, in order to gain respectability. And there is a certain kudos to Otherworldly encounters that may encourage dramatization. Because the subject is extremely confusing, people involved in fairy incidents have a tendency to behave irrationally and inconsistently. This is not really very surprising, as fairies are usually mischievous creatures and are likely to bring muddles in their wake!

The Cottingley encounter was documented in 1997 in *The Case of the Cottingley Fairies* by Joe Cooper and was turned into the film *Fairy Story*. But were there really fairies in the beck at Cottingley? If so, they should still be there, accessible to anyone with the innocent heart and clear eyes of a child.

The Fairies of Findhorn

The modern idea of nature spirits arose principally from the experiences of a community in Findhorn, Scotland, where they grew wonderful plants in barren soil. The full account of how this happened is described in To Hear the Angels Sing, an Odyssey of Co-creation with the Devic Kingdom *by Dorothy Maclean (1990).*

B y a series of coincidences, Dorothy and her friends Eileen and Peter Caddy found themselves down and out in a caravan site at Findhorn Bay, not far from the Moray Firth. Their caravan was surrounded by plants such as gorse that could survive in the stony

soil. Traditional stories told how a local laird had sold his soul to the Devil, and because of this, the land was covered with gale-driven silt. The winter was bitter and the winds perpetual. However, when spring came, Peter began to work the soil to grow food.

Dorothy was in the habit of meditating, and began to receive messages about harmonizing with the forces of Nature. She was told that if humans tried to tune into the spirits of Nature, they would receive help from the higher spirits, and from the smaller "nature spirits" under their direction. So, because she liked eating peas, she began with the pea spirit.

Realizing that she was in contact with creatures of joy and light, Dorothy used the Sanskrit term *deva*—meaning "shining one"—for them. She had contact with a spirit that she called the Landscape Angel, and it gradually dawned on the three friends that life is an energy network directed by such beings. The garden at Findhorn flourished, and when the soil was scientifically tested, it was found to have a good balance of nutrients, in contrast to the soil around it. Findhorn is now an established community attracting people who are spiritually inclined. It seems that it was a kind of "pilot scheme" on behalf of the devas, showing humans what can be done when the forces of Nature are cooperated with by humans and guided by love.

Tranquillity results from appreciating that we are a part of the oneness of the Universe, which surrounds and informs nature spirits and all that they do. Devas use mantras and sounds, producing patterns and raising vibrations; they are part of each specific place's essence. If we can expand our minds to appreciate that existence is a network of vibration, we can return to instinctual wisdom and learn to live in harmony with Nature. To paraphrase T.S. Eliot, we shall keep exploring, and at the end of exploration we shall find ourselves back where we started, but able now to see clearly.

Sources of Fairy Lore

Traditionally, the sources of fairy lore have always been people who lived close to the land and interacted with fairies. Contrary to what we may assume, psychic powers are not confined to darkened rooms. In fact, the best way to boost your intuition and gain "the sight" is to be out in Nature, where the Otherworld is always close. The Irish poet W.B. Yeats was very clear on the subject: fairies are seen by farmers and woodsmen, and not necessarily by poets and artists.

M any fairies are the very breath of the land itself and are linked to the essence of place. The concept of the fairy belongs largely to Western perceptions, and while all cultures have their fairy traditions, these often combine and merge with ideas about gods and ancestors. Although to some extent this has been true in the West, our idea of a fairy is generally closer to a "nature spirit," and for this there are several principal bodies of lore, which we shall explore.

TRUE THOMAS

Thomas the Rhymer's encounter with fairies is a classic in fairy annals. His actual name was Thomas Rymour of Erceldoune, and he was also called True Thomas. He dwelt in 13th-century Scotland, and while his story is held to be true, it has naturally been embellished. It has come down to us in two poems: first, the "Romance," which was written within a century of his death and may be partly his own work; and secondly, the "Ballad," which is more fictional and was written in the 19th century. The latter recounts

how the Queen of Elfland fell in love with Thomas, and how he experienced her dark and terrible side as well as her sensuous, magical self. She carried Thomas away into the land of the fairies, releasing him only when the seven-yearly tribute to the Devil was due and she feared that Thomas might be chosen. Thomas was released back into the human realm, with the gift of the "sight" and a tongue that could not lie. He became famous throughout

OTHER INFLUENTIAL WRITINGS

Robert Kirk, a Scottish minister living between 1644 and 1692, wrote a definitive guide to the beliefs of the Highlanders entitled *The Secret Commonwealth of Elves, Fauns and Fairies*. He described fairy lovers, co-walkers, and many other fairy secrets. When he was found dead beside the Fairy Knowe at Aberfoyle, the locals said that his corpse was not real, but a fairy substitute or "stock," and that Kirk had been abducted by the fairies. Kirk later appeared to his cousin and told him he was a prisoner in Fairyland, and that when his posthumous child was christened, this cousin should throw his dirk (dagger) over his ghostly form to free him. Kirk duly materialized at the christening, but the cousin lost his chance and the minister remained a prisoner. Hope for Kirk's release lived on into the 20th century, and his chair still stands in the manse in Aberfoyle.

Scotland, but his heart remained in the land of Fairy. One day, when feasting with friends, word came that a hart and a hind were walking openly up the street. Thomas rose without a word and followed the animals into the forest, never to be seen again. However, those who journey into Fairyland in states of meditation may report encounters with Thomas, as a mentor on the subtle planes.

George William Russell, the seer known as A.E., was a 19th-century Irishman who, despite being a poet and psychic, was also an eminently pragmatic economist and expert on agriculture. His accounts of fairies, in prose and painting, describe them clearly as shining beings that draw energy from the earth. These beings equate with the pre-Celtic people of the Sidhe (pronounced *shee*), who slid into another dimension as humans took over the land. A.E.'s work is influential on the subject of fairy lore because he presented it in ways that were acceptable and inspiring to his contemporaries and posterity.

A definitive body of evidence was compiled by W.Y. Evans Wentz at the turn of the 20th century, entitled *The Fairy Faith in Celtic Countries*. At this time the existence of fairies was widely accepted, probably as a survival of what had once been a universal belief. This work comprises many anecdotes from Scotland, Ireland, Wales, Cornwall, Brittany, and the Isle of Man, and much of what we "know" about fairies is detailed in this book.

Fairies may be offended by disrespectful prying and may be scornful of mistaken assumptions. The truest knowledge of fairies always comes through an open heart.

Why Invite Fairies into Your Life?

The stresses of modern life are well known, and yet they are increasing with every year that passes. "We have no time to stand and stare" at the world about us, as the Welsh poet W.H. Davies noted, or even to be aware of our own true nature, feelings, and preferences. The seasons mean little to us in our centrally heated homes.

Who needs to worry about the harvest, when the local supermarket shelves are heaving with produce from around the globe? Who can be bothered to marvel at a wood carpeted with bluebells, when many flowers—forced into unnatural growth—can be so easily bought all year round? Who grows their own herbs, watches the Moon's phases or sniffs the air for an approaching storm? Perhaps vaguely, perhaps even quite sharply, we know something is missing, but it is hard to know what to do about it—so often we do nothing.

Of course, we would not want to be without the gifts that modern life provides—but are we aware of the price we have paid, and are continuing to pay? We are often stranded in our thoughts, alienated from the ground of our own being. Many people feel that life is meaningless, despite having so many comforts. Depression is common because it is so hard to feel part of anything that inspires us with wonder. For many people, the established religions have lost their appeal, because their dogmas seem irrelevant. Life can seem a little empty.

TO RENEW YOUR ACQUAINTANCE WITH NATURE

Not so very long ago, people had no choice but to be aware of Nature and her powers, because their very lives depended on it. In ages past, the natural world was seen as being animated by spirits—gods and goddesses who needed to be kept happy in order that the streams might fill with salmon, the trees might fruit, and the lake water might remain pure for drinking. Meadow, grove, river, mountain— all of these were alive, peopled with wonderful, subtle beings, who (with any luck) would give a helping hand to humans who asked them nicely. That way of thinking about the world may seem illogical to modern consciousness, but even science is a way of "thinking about the world." It gives us the answers to lots of things, but not everything. It does not give us a sense of wonderment, of belonging, within a vibrant, amazing world. Maybe people who lived close to Nature knew a thing or two that we have chosen to forget?

However, we can "remember" it, by renewing our acquaintance and respect for fairies. These beings are often the very essence of the natural world, in one form or another. By opening ourselves to them we can find a different perspective on our own existence. This is all about feelings and

it is hard to put into words. But the gifts of fairies are many and varied, and in their company the world becomes so much more than simply a machine grinding on, or myriads of atoms spinning in their predetermined course. It becomes something with soul.

TO LEARN TO RELAX AND CONNECT

Fairies can help you not only to see Nature, but also to experience it, in your heart. Like the poet William Wordsworth, you may see the world "apparelled in celestial light"—or you may simply feel that your being has expanded, that you can relax and feel "at home." Of course, these days we can afford to be sentimental about Nature, seeing only the beautiful and nurturing

side, and for the most part forgetting its destructive side. There is no harm in being positive about things, but it must be said that fairies can also show us the negative, and enable us to feel real respect for powers that are beyond our ability to control.

Fairies are our connection with Nature, but they bring many other gifts too. They can help enhance your imagination and your creativity. They can help you to relax, and to laugh, in the certain knowledge that nothing really matters *that much*. Fairies have seen it all come and go! If you are going wrong, they can nudge you in the right direction; if you are bogged down, they can free you up and give you a sense of possibilities; if you are sad, they can promise hope and consolation; and if you are disappointed, they can brighten your life with their magic.

What are you waiting for? Lace up your walking boots, get down to the woods and get close to the fairies.

Sensing the Presence of Fairies

Becoming aware of the presence of fairies involves tuning into parts of yourself that you may have learnt to ignore. It means trusting your instincts, and being relaxed. It is not a good idea to go "hunting" for fairies exactly, because that means that you are trying too hard. More importantly, you would be focusing your intellect on achieving a specific goal, and that kind of thing can make fairies uncooperative and even mischievous.

Naturally, you want to be aware of the Fair Folk, and there are many ways to invite them close to you. Preserve a playful attitude, to keep your senses open. Use your imagination to start with. Where do you imagine would be the best place to feel the presence of fairies? Is there some special dell, grassy bank, flowerbed, or tree where it seems to you they could well linger? Chances are you are correct in what you imagine, because your subconscious mind has already picked up the fact that fairies are there.

"IN-BETWEEN" LOCATIONS AND TIMES

Traditionally, fairies are believed to favor the "places in between." At these sites there is a shift in the energy pattern, which makes them more suitable for fairies. And fairies are "in-between" creatures, for although they are spirit beings, they are also close to the earth. At the "in-between" places there is plenty for a fairy to attend to. Such locations include crossroads, especially on country roads and lanes, hedgerows and fences, woodland glades, bends in the road, and bridges. Other fairy sites are the seashore; beside a lake or by a stream, especially where a stream divides into two; by fountains and waterfalls; beside rockpools left by the tide; and on small islands. In your house, fairies are most likely to linger near the threshold, in the hall or on the stairs or landing, and sometimes in cupboards and corners.

It will probably feel more inspiring to seek fairies outside, for within your house you have probably fallen into habit patterns that make this more difficult. Nature has a way of reaching into your soul and opening it. The best times for fairy encounters are, appropriately, the "in-between" times of dusk, dawn, midday, and midnight. Fairies also love the moonlight. Certain times of year, when the season is on the change, are also fairy favorites. This will be examined more closely on pages 62–77 where we look at fairy festivals. There are many seasonal shift-points:

have you ever found yourself thinking, "Aah! Today spring has really begun!" or smelt the first scent of autumn on the breeze? Those are fairy times, but of all of them, the Autumn Equinox (around September 21 in the Northern Hemisphere and March 21 in the Southern Hemisphere) is the moment when the veil between this world and the Otherworld is at its thinnest.

LEARNING JUST TO "BE"

When it feels right and you are able to be relaxed, go to a special place of your choice and just "be" there at first. Don't try too hard; simply unwind. Be very aware of your body, for often intuition speaks through bodily sensations that you may do your best to ignore. Do you feel hot or chilled? Is your tummy fluttering? Are your limbs tingling or your palms itching? Can you feel a breeze, a tickle, or a twitch? Simply note anything that you feel, without making judgments.

Note also your emotions. Do you feel contented, joyful, or expansive? Or a little uneasy, as if you are being watched. Or do you feel a mixture of these? Again, use your imagination. If fairies are here, what might they look like? Whatever pops into your mind is likely to be your intuition breaking through once more. As you start to be aware of fairies, you will probably begin to notice movement out of the corner of your eye, only to see nothing when you turn. Learn not to turn—remember, just "be."

Fairies may also show themselves through a whisper in the leaves, a movement in the grass, a ripple in the water, a breathless stillness in the air, and through strange losses of time. They can also give you the giggles! Sensing fairies is not about proving that they are there—it is about feeling uplifted, entranced and a little excited about life. Feel these things and you may be sure the fairies have been close by.

Reaching Out to Fairies

Many fairies are understandably wary of human beings. We are the ones who are messing up the planet that they so lovingly tend—and we are the ones who say they do not exist. Fairies can be shy, grumpy, teasing, and aloof, and often they simply don't care very much about us. It is up to us to prove that we have something to offer.

Any living being wants love and respect, and to offer that is a great way to become acquainted with fairies. Nature spirits will be drawn to you if you tend a patch of ground with love. Spending time in Nature, especially if you return again and again to the same spot, will give the message to the fairies that inhabit it that you are interested, and respectful. One especially fairy-friendly act is to reclaim a derelict and neglected spot, gathering up litter, unblocking a stream, or clearing weeds and brambles. The spirits of the place are likely to bless you for this. By contrast, letting a patch of your garden grow wild will also invite fairies to come and play there. The Fair Folk, in general, will appreciate it if you are aware of the abuses of the natural world and do your best to improve things, by recycling, reusing, and generally doing your best to live in a way that is friendly to the environment.

They are also drawn to people who are generous, truthful, and honorable.

Household fairies respond to some loving care. Housework isn't a "fashionable" occupation, but fairies do not like a dingy, cluttered, and dirty house. Scrubbing like mad isn't called for, but a little effort, a bit of polishing and rearranging can encourage their presence. Behave as if they are there—talk to them and ask for their help. Fairies are attracted to houseplants, so make room for a few of these and treat them lovingly. In the garden, fairies will make your roses bloom luxuriantly, while in the kitchen they will make your cakes rise. Always leave a small offering of food outside on the earth for the fairies, at the end of any special meal. They will not take the food (at least not usually), but they will absorb its essence and appreciate your thoughtful actions.

Creativity is a magnet for the fairies. You do not have to be especially talented to please them; just enjoy it. Playing an instrument, painting, drawing, knitting, writing poetry, cooking—these and many more activities will attract them. Singing is especially wonderful. Keep the child in you alive and the fairies will flock.

USE MEDITATION TO DRAW CLOSE

Meditating in one of the "in-between" places already described is likely to shift your consciousness to the fairy level. More detailed instructions for meditation are given later in the book. Meditation begins by being relaxed and allowing yourself to drift into a daydream state. It may help you to look into a stream or lake, or to fix your eyes on a flower, leaf, or patch of sunlight. You may also have a special symbol that means peace to you, such as a circle or star, so concentrate on that if you wish. As your meditation deepens, so your proximity to the fairies will grow. Sometimes you will receive a fairy gift,

such as a feather brought by a wind sprite, or a whiff of alluring fragrance from a flower fairy; a bird may draw close to you, to sing especially for you; or you may discover a special stone or shell. Fairies may also inspire other people to give you items such as crystals or plants.

Try to understand what the fairies want by sitting and noting what comes into your mind, as already described (see page 27). If you are dressed in natural materials, such as cotton and wool, so much the better. Avoid wearing metals (especial iron), for some fairies don't like them (silver, gold, and crystals are another matter). Ask the fairies what they want—either mentally or out loud. You may "hear" a voice in your head, or you may suddenly feel sure what they require. If you are really talented, you may be spoken to by a silvery voice that leaves you in no doubt. Do your best to provide whatever they request, because it will create a bond between you.

How to Use this Book

The realm of the fairies is elusive and inspiring. It isn't something that lends itself to an intellectual approach. You do not need to learn and remember lots of information about fairies in order to be aware of them and benefit from their presence. For this reason it may be best to dip into this book, as the fancy takes you, letting your intuition— and the fairies themselves—guide you to pages that are relevant to you at the moment.

This book is intended to be a companion, a working guide, and a source of information. It is a good idea to familiarize yourself with this Introduction and with The Realm of Fairies (see pages 42–101), especially if the world of fairies is new to you. These sections give you some background, and help attune you to the fairy realm. Later in the book there are specific meditations, spells, and healing exercises, which you should choose according to what feels right for you. You do not have to work through them in sequence, like a textbook, unless you have a very orderly mind and can only be satisfied that way.

A VOYAGE OF DISCOVERY

There is no dogma in these pages. This guide is intended to be as comprehensive as possible, but to claim to be definitive would be to show disrespect to the delicacy of fairies. Besides, you will make your own relationship with the fairies, and no book (however well written) can describe exactly how that will occur, any more than looking at a map can give you experience of a landscape.

Perhaps the best way to regard this book is as a portal. Let it open you to the discovery of new worlds and novel experiences. Make a little ritual out of consulting it, if you like, by lighting a candle or burning aromatic oils to help your consciousness shift. Try to feel calm whenever you touch it, for in that way you will more easily go into that dreamy state of mind where fairies draw close. Best of all, wrap the book up and put it in your backpack when you go on country rambles. With a bit of luck and a sprinkle of magic dust, you will need to consult it about the fairies that you meet on your path.

Learning to Relax

In order to make the best use of the meditation exercises in this book, you will need to be able to relax, both physically and mentally. This will be highly beneficial in itself. And being able to relax is also the best preparation you can have for contact with fairies, because tension is the major barrier between this world and the Otherworld.

When you feel relaxed, you will be able to go on inward journeys more readily, and paradoxically these can also be journeys to the Otherworld. Like so many things, relaxation is largely a matter of habit. Tell yourself that you will put aside ten minutes each day to relax, in order to get the message through to your subconscious. Try to do this at the same time each day, and make sure that no one and nothing disturbs you.

THE RELAXATION PROCESS

Lie on the bed, for that immediately suggests relaxation. Bring your awareness to your body, and mentally check over all your muscles. Imagine a feeling of warmth starting at the crown of your head and flowing down over all the tiny muscles in your scalp, face, and neck, taking away all tension as it moves. Feel it passing over your shoulders, arms, hands, and fingers. Then it flows down your chest and abdomen, down your back and spine, and all around your pelvis. Finally, it travels gently down your legs, ankles, heels, feet, and toes, leaving you feeling relaxed and "floaty."

If you prefer, you can tense each muscle in turn, starting with your toes and working slowly and thoroughly up

your legs and torso, into your shoulders, arms, hands and fingers, then into your neck, jaw, head, and face. After tensing, relax each muscle completely. Work through your body twice, being careful to avoid getting cramp by not tensing the muscles too much.

Let thoughts drift in and out of your head—they are not important. Let yourself become absorbed in feeling relaxed. Soon a sensation of well-being will be present, and you will be ready to start your meditation. The best idea is to record your visualization onto a tape, so that you can listen to it effortlessly and travel into your own inner magical world.

Regular relaxing, listening, traveling, and experiencing is likely to have a knock-on effect, making you more serene in everyday life and getting things into proportion—your first gift from the fairies.

Getting Organized

Drawing close to the fairies is a spiritual matter, but a little practicality and planning will be very helpful.

First, make sure you have some decent walking boots, so that you can ramble in remote, fairy-haunted spots. The boots should be well-fitting and as waterproof as possible—sneakers won't suffice for long walks in rough or rocky country. Wear your boots in before relying on them for extensive rambles. Of course, fairies can also be found close to home, even in your own house and garden, but if you want to wander, get some boots.

CREATE A DEVOTIONAL ALTAR

In your home, set aside a shelf or cupboard top as a devotional space, or altar, for the fairies (specific suggestions are given in each section on different types of fairy). An altar does not have to be about dogmatic religious belief—it is merely a center for observance and helps to keep your mind focused. It also affirms that fairies are "special" and that you are making room for them in your life. A selection of candles and joss-sticks and/or an oil burner and some essential oils will be handy for your altar.

Collect artifacts that appeal to you and that strike you as having a fairy ambience. Crystals are an obvious choice, but you may find many items on walks that seem like gifts from the fairies, such as special stones, feathers, twigs in cunning shapes, or even old keys, coins, and bits of jewelry. Fairies can sometimes inhabit objects—for instance, a much-loved teddy bear may have an occupying spirit. Anything that you feel is suitable can go on your altar, if you wish.

MAKE VISUAL AND WRITTEN RECORDS

Start a fairy scrapbook. This is not simply a collector's hobby, but a matter of putting together all the fairy reminders that you come across. These may include pictures, poems, pressed leaves and flowers, cuttings, photos— anything, in fact. Soon you will probably find that you encounter more and more things for your scrapbook, as your mind tunes in.

Most important of all, make sure that you have a notebook in which to record all your feelings and thoughts about the fairies. When you practice the guided visualizations given later in the book, you will be reminded to write down all your experiences. This will build into your own personal treasury of fairy lore, to enrich your life.

Protection from Bad Fairies

By no means are all fairies well disposed towards humans. This does not mean that they are evil—just that they have different standards of morality from us. Fairies may regard as important things that have nothing to do with the welfare of humankind, and such matters may be very necessary in the scheme of things. For instance, there is a place in the world for poisonous plants, just as death and decay have a purpose. Fairies may be linked with these natural processes, but we do not want to go looking for them.

F airies have been credited with kidnapping the young, beautiful, or talented – especially those who were musically talented. Young mothers were also fair game, because they could suckle fairy babies. And babies themselves were very much at risk, particularly before they were baptized. Fairies were believed to take the real person and leave a "stock," or fairy double, in their place. In the case of a child, this was termed a "changeling." Most sinister of all, fairies were

believed to take
humans for tribute to the Devil.

Another nasty fairy habit was
believed to be that of shooting "elf-
shot" at certain people, or at cattle.
These were flint arrowheads, and the
person or beast struck would develop
some ailment. A certain type of fairy,
known as a "joint-eater," may also
attach itself to a person and absorb all
the goodness from the food they eat, so
that the unfortunate human is always
ravenous and undernourished.

Fairies credited with malevolence
are too numerous to list, but they
include goblins, hobgoblins, the Kelpie,
(who appears as a horse and lures
weary travelers onto its back so that it
may ride them into deep water and
drown them) and the Phooka (who also
appears as a very nasty horse and may
spoil crops). Some fairies can be vicious
and malevolent, and indeed all may be
capricious and tricky. "Fairy terror"
may assail anyone who is out on their
own in the wild.

THE CHURCH VERSUS FAIRIES

Much of the bad press suffered by fairies is connected with a dogmatic type of Christianity, which regards anything that is not of the Christian God as evil. There is a tendency to polarize, and to regard anything that is not totally "good" as totally "bad." The Universe isn't like that (ask any fairy). Fear of the Church during and after the Middle Ages gave rise to a great deal of fearful and condemnatory attitude towards fairies. In fact, the Devil is a Christian concept, while fairies are far older than Christianity and have been with the earth for aeons. In pagan times, the nature spirits were honored, but when Christianity took over, the gods of the old religion became the devils of the new, leaving fairies in a kind of unhallowed limbo. That is very sad, because fairies love the earth, and the earth is mother to us all.

Having said all this, there are times when you may—just may—need some protection against fairies. On the rare occasion when you sense a powerfully evil presence in a place, *leave that place and stay away*. For those times when keeping away is not a practical option you could carry a protective talisman (see opposite).

PROTECTIVE TALISMANS

If you experience fairy terror, try not to run away, because you are likely to get entangled in brambles and become lost. But do not trespass where you feel unwelcome. Remain calm, leave slowly and send out love as an offering. Traditional fairy deterrents include the cross and holy water (if you believe fairies are satanic), but more natural protection comes from carrying a daisy, St. John's wort, a rowan twig, or a four-leafed clover. All these, in their different ways, symbolize the balance of Nature.

Most useful of all, practice visualizing a protective egg of golden light surrounding your body. This egg enables you to radiate love outward, but lets nothing negative penetrate its shell. You may also pick a symbol that you visualize (something that is especially meaningful for you) or carry a talisman of your own (which could be anything from a pressed flower to your old teddy bear). The point is that this talisman is infused with positive energy. Spend time imagining your golden sheath and visualizing your protective symbol held up before you—do this for a few minutes each day and it will come readily to you, should you need it.

Arm yourself with love and empower yourself with positive thought. Go in good faith, and the fairies will welcome you.

The Realm of Fairies

Where is the Realm of Fairies?

Where is Fairyland? Here, there … somewhere … It is just around the corner, under a rosebush, in a hollow tree; deep in the moonlit forest, veiled by the morning mist that hangs over the meadow—fairies inhabit another dimension, but it is not so far from our own. In fact, it is very close. Their world interpenetrates ours, but because it vibrates at a different frequency, it is glimpsed only at certain times and places, by the fortunate and gifted.

There are many traditions about Fairyland. Some say it lies in the Hollow Hills, the prehistoric tumuli of Ireland, to which the pre-Celtic beings, the Tuatha de Danann, departed. These creatures were also known as the people of the Sidhe—*Sidhe* meaning a hill or a mound, as well as supernatural. Fairyland may also be at the bottom of a lake, where these magical beings retreated. Sometimes the realm of fairies was found on mountain peaks, on moorland, or in forest clearings. The gates of Fairyland might appear and open wide to some people, while remaining totally invisible to others.

THE PARADISE OF TIR-NAN-OG

Another Celtic concept of the Land of the Fairies was Tir-nan-Og, meaning "The Land of the Young." This paradise lay across the sea, to the west. In this deathless land of romance and dancing, all was beautiful, the grass forever green and the trees perpetually laden with fruit and flowers.

There are certain spots on the earth that we register as magical. We may know of hauntings reported there. Often these places are marked by a standing stone or by strange trees, and frequently they are near water. Within houses and other buildings we may also be aware of "cold spots," where the hairs on the backs of our necks seem to rise. Certain places have a sinister feel and are best avoided. Others mark a point where, for some mysterious reason, this world can intersect with the realm of the fairies.

There is one place, however, where Fairyland can always be found, and that is within your own heart. Keep this special place pure and light, and the gates to Fairyland will always be open to you.

Special Fairy Realms

The spiritual realms have many levels, all of them inhabited by beings. Some are close to this earth, such as Tir-nan-Og; others are too rarefied for us to imagine; many others lie in between. We may travel to such places at night, while sleeping, when we are in what occultists term our "astral body." This is a subtle, spirit body that exists in the same space as our flesh-and-blood body, but during slumber it separates. It remains connected to the body by a silver cord, but is able to travel far, far away from it, in this world or the Otherworld. So we can visit the fairy realms in our dreams.

Many things that we learn about Fairyland, and about the activities of fairies, do not slot neatly together. Partly this is because our view of existence as having to "fit together" is a product of our rationalism. Fairies and Fairyland are notoriously irrational and inconsistent, and yet there are patterns with which we can become familiar, if we put our trust in our instincts and perceptions.

THE FOUR ELEMENTS

When a belief or concept runs deep within the human psyche, the chances are that it has a reality on the "astral planes," for these are formed in part from our imagination, and/or it is our imagination that is formed from them. One of the ideas that has run deeply and persistently through Western occultism is that of the four Elements: Air, Fire, Water, and Earth. The ancients believed literally that all substance was made of these. More symbolically, these Elements have powerful meanings and are associated with basic energies, which we may call on or be called by. Fairies are associated with these Elements, and many fairies are specifically grouped as belonging to a particular Element. These will be explored in their own sections later in this book.

On one level of the astral plane, there are four wonderful fairy cities, each associated with a specific Element: Air, Fire, Water, or Earth. In turn, these are linked with East, South, West, and North respectively. These are, in a sense, mysterious portals for the elemental energies, as they enter our level of existence. They are also the dwellings of certain fairy beings who are most at home there, or of those who, for their own purposes, wish to visit. You can also visit them while dreaming, or through visualizing.

THE FAIRY CITY OF GORIAS

Gorias is the city of Air and the East. Here a crystal stream, fed by many glittering cascades falling from dizzy pinnacles, winds through an emerald valley. Rectangular white buildings cling to the sides of the surrounding mountains, with multicolored pennants streaming out from their rooftops and fluttering in the perpetual breeze. In the valley stands a square building with a gleaming roof of pure gold. An atmosphere of peace and tranquillity pervades, flowers grow in brilliant profusion, and the fields are full of smiling workers.

Within the gold-capped building, embroidered hangings display creatures of beauty, terror, and enchantment. Deeper inside, in a shadowy chamber, stands a statue of solid gold. So pure is this gold that its radiance lights the room. The statue is of a man with a drawn sword in his right hand and a flower in his left. This statue is, in fact, the fairy teacher of this land. The sword he holds represents the power of the intellect to cut through ignorance. The flower indicates that this is tempered by gentleness. Air is the Element most associated with thought.

THE FAIRY CITY OF FINIAS

Finias is the city of Fire and the South. Sun-baked sands stretch into the distance, and on an oasis stands a group of ancient buildings. Straddled by an impressive archway, a road heads into the desert, only to disintegrate to rubble on the arid earth. Silvery trees shade the oasis, and the people are warm-hearted. Here light is perpetual; night never descends. The road heads into the heart of the city, toward an ancient and decrepit building, covered with arcane symbols.

The inside of this building is cool and welcoming. On the floor there is a spiral, and when you tread on it you are filled with the urge to dance and become part of the web of life. In a farther windowless room, a staff is planted in the floor. It grows branches and blossoms while you watch. Beautiful scents fill the room, and all things seem possible. The fairy teacher of Finias imparts that all is indeed possible—if you wish it to be so—for Fire is the Element most associated with imagination and intuition. You are invited to be part of its vibrancy.

THE FAIRY CITY OF MURIAS

Murias is the city of Water and the West. It stands on the shores of a western ocean, and behind it the hills rise, low and undulating. Raindrops blow in on the wind, making the cobbled streets glisten in the evening sun. Tradespeople are busy selling lush fruits and sumptuous fabrics, and many fair ships, laden with foreign produce, sway at anchor in the harbor. Luxuriant trees grow among the red-tiled buildings, their leaves turning to rich shades of russet and gold as autumn approaches.

A great cathedral stands on a rise, with a path leading to its western door. Its dim interior is resplendent with strange carvings, speaking of ineffable wisdom. At the far end, a wonderful rose window shines in the dying sunlight. As you watch, this marvelous window begins to glow and bloom as if it is a real rose. Your heart blossoms in response. On the altar you notice a perfect golden chalice. The fairy teacher of Murias seeks to open your heart to your own feelings and those of others, for Water is the Element of emotion.

THE FAIRY CITY OF FALIAS

Falias is the city of Earth and the North. It is approached in all-pervading darkness. Its towers are made of metal and topped by brilliant jewels that glow like beacons. The city is massive and solid. There are no inhabitants, but it breathes of rich life, for it is the blueprint of all earthly cities, and it seems familiar.

In the center of the city stands a huge piece of meteoric rock, around which there hangs an aura of the unutterably ancient. A subtle light plays around the stone, and with it comes a multitude of memories, of this world and the Otherworld, of the personal and the collective, and there is an awareness of countless lifetimes and of the deep wisdom inherent within the city. The fairy teacher of Falias wishes you to be aware of your connection with the earth and to touch this rock, thus becoming aware of the ancientness of your soul, for Earth is the Element connected with reality and experience, and with the source of being.

Fairy Landscapes, Rings, and Paths

There are countless signs of fairies in Nature, and these often exist close to or within areas that are quite built up. You will soon come to recognize them intuitively. Wherever there is a strangely twisted tree, a tufted hillock, a pile of pebbles, or a cluster of wild flowers, there you may detect fairy workings. Be aware of unusual features or anything that looks mysterious, and especially of any place that feels as if it has its own "atmosphere"—that will be because of the fairies. Feast your eyes on meadows filled with buttercups, daisies, and emerald grass, reedy river banks and bluebell woods, knowing that the fairies are close by.

FAIRY RINGS

One natural feature that has been especially credited to fairies is the "fairy ring." This is a circle of darker-colored grass, caused by the outward spread of a fungus. However, this is not the only type of ring that you will find in Nature, if you explore. Crop circles are a well-known natural phenomenon, but other vegetation (including grass) can also be found bent into a ring formation. Moss may grow in a circle, and trees may leave clear a patch of ground that is more or less circular. All these places are fairy haunts, where the Good Folk do what they so love to

do—dance. Tales are told of travelers who were led by sweet music into such a ring, whereupon they disappeared from sight, lost to the realm of Fairy. If you meditate within such a ring, you are more likely to be in tune with the fairies.

FAIRY PATHS

Fairy pathways may often be encountered. They might be narrow trails, apparently starting nowhere in particular and either ending abruptly or going toward a stone or mound that has no obvious use. Such paths are the sign of an interface between this world and the Otherworld. Spirit beings walk upon them and are more readily glimpsed in such places, especially if you do not stare directly at the path, but walk alongside it, aware of what you see from the corner of your eye. Such paths exist within dwellings too, and it may be along them that "ghosts" are seen to walk, apparently vanishing where the path—and the link between the worlds—ends.

Fairy Food and Drink

It has long been known that to eat or drink food offered by the fairies,
when one is in their land, is very dangerous. Such fare appears
delicious, but it is not "real" food by our standards. It is just fairy
"glamour" and may have no true substance, or may be, in effect,
simply weeds and pebbles. When reaching out for the tempting
platter, the enchanted traveler may have a harsh awakening. Worse
still, if fairy food is eaten (and presumably found to be really
palatable), the person remains for ever captive with the fairies.

Food, of course, is energy—and fairy energy is not the same as human energy. What is food to fairies cannot actually nourish our physical bodies, for they are of another substance. In fact, to try to eat fairy-stuff is to attempt to reduce the magical to the commonplace—small wonder that it brings unhappiness. The case of those, in legend, who did eat fairy food was obviously different, for if they succeeded in consuming it, they had themselves become the very essence of Fairyland and could not return to the land of the living. Traditionally, there was always a taboo against eating anything if one was taken by the fairies. Sometimes fairies may even steal the essential nourishment from human food, leaving it worthless, although it may seem the same. Fairies may also wash their feet in milk or wine, if a house they visit is not clean and running water is unavailable.

The fairy attitude to food is capricious and Otherworldly.

THANK OFFERINGS

Not everything concerning fairies and food is negative, however. Fairies have been known to give delectable cakes to humans to thank them for their help, and these can be eaten with no harm at all, as in the case of the kind ploughman on Wick Moor, who mended a fairy's spade and was given such a reward. And Scottish fairies would sometimes borrow human food—usually their favorite grain, which was barley (possibly because it is sacred to the love goddess Venus)—and would then give back double the amount, as a thank-you.

Best of all, the good Brownies help friendly humans with their kitchen tasks. In return, they appreciate a bowl of milk and a cake, especially one made with honey—not too much to ask. Next time you are too tired to wash up, leave an offering out for the Brownies—you never know!

Fairy Clothes

Clothes are no small matter to fairies, who realize that clothing says a
great deal about the wearer and has symbolic meanings. Some fairies
prefer to remain naked, in the same way that some modern-day pagans,
within closed rituals, prefer to be "sky-clad." They feel this is a sign
that we are all naked before the gods, and shows respect for Nature.

CLOTHES AS A SIGN OF POWER

By contrast, other fairy folk are very fussy about clothing, preferring the beautiful and the costly. In many cultures, clothes define the status and occupation of the wearer, and so are an outward sign of an inward reality. We are freed from such constraints in the modern world, but fairies are well aware of the symbolic nature of all things. Some fairies, robbed of their clothing, are doomed to remain captive in the mortal world until they recover it. The good Persian fairy, the Peri, is one example, whose clothes signify her magical power.

One story tells of a weary merchant's son, who rested from his travels by the shores of a lake. Four doves flew down and turned into Peries before his eyes. They then shed their robes and bathed in the waters. The young man hid the clothes and, when they realized what had happened, the Peries were distraught. One of them agreed to marry him in order that the others might escape, whereupon he gave three Peries back their clothes, taking the fourth with him as his bride. They lived together for ten years, after which he went on his travels again, leaving the precious clothes with an old woman. When he was gone, the

Peri persuaded the old woman to let her put her clothes on just for a minute—whereupon she immediately vanished from sight.

Many fairies are intentionally ragged in appearance, such as the Brownies. However, if they are given clothes, they are so offended that they often disappear for ever. This idea is echoed by J.K. Rowling in the Harry Potter books, in which a house elf is freed by the gift of clothes. To traditional house fairies, clothes are an empty gift conforming to human standards, not to those of Fairyland.

THE SIGNIFICANCE OF COLOR

Color is also an important consideration, with red and green being favorites. Both of these colors speak of the power of Nature: red being the color of blood (and of death, with which some fairies are linked), and green the color of leaves and grass. Irish Leprechauns usually wear green, along with leather aprons, silver-buckled shoes, and three-cornered hats, on which they may turn upside down and spin. In fact, in Ireland green is so

be associated with shamanism and with the fly agaric mushroom, which induces a trance (see page 81).

CLOTHES AS SYMBOLS

Human clothes can also be used as a weapon to break fairy enchantment. When led astray by fairies while out walking (that is, "pixy-led"), the best thing to do is to take off your coat and turn it inside out, thus distracting the fairies long enough to escape. This may also be a way of marshalling all the powers of your conscious mind so that you can think logically.

much the property of the Fair Folk that it may be unlucky for mortals to wear it. Some fairies even have green skin. Nature spirits are the types of fairy most closely linked to green and the world of vegetation.

Red has magical connections, and witches are believed by some to have red hair and to wear red cloaks or caps. Red is also linked with death, and in prehistoric times corpses were often smeared with red ochre, to give them renewed vitality. And the sun, when it "dies," goes down in a blaze of red. Many fairies have red caps, or are entirely red in color. Red caps may also

If troublesome fairies are disturbing your nights, place your shoes by the bed with the toes pointing outward and put your socks beneath them. Gloves are even more important as symbols. A glove thrown into a fairy ring will stop all the revelry, and one Cornish tale describes how a farmer called Noy threw down his glove at a fairy assembly, whereupon the entire company disappeared, along with the house and orchard. Many customs feature gloves, as a sign of intention or authority—"throwing down the gauntlet," for instance, was a medieval challenge, accepted if the gauntlet was picked up. The human hand has been the tool that has wrought many changes in the natural world—small

wonder that the fairies are alive to the meaning of the glove.

Nothing is just what it seems: All things have a meaning beyond their purpose, and naught more so than clothes. If humans will not realize this, the fairies will teach them.

Fairy Music and Language

Fairies love music above all things, for it embodies vibration and harmony, which are the essence of creation, and has the ability to link all levels of being. It may also change levels of consciousness, which is one of the reasons why contact with fairies often begins by hearing their melodies. Mermaids are credited with having voices so enchanting that sailors and coastal wanderers might be lured by them to their deaths. However, mermaids are connected to the unconscious and to feelings, and if we respect these, we are likely to find them inspiring rather than dangerous.

HISTORICAL ACCOUNTS

Gifted musicians are favored by the fairies, who may try to spirit them back to Fairyland, to play for them at their revels. Thomas the Rhymer, for instance, was lured away by the Fairy Queen because he was a fine poet and musician (see page 17). Musicians who are able to listen to the music of the fairies are especially inspired. And there are pieces of music in existence that are reputed to be of fairy origin, such as the "Londonderry Air" and "The Fairy Dance of Scotland."

The English antiquary John Aubrey, who lived from 1626 to 1697 near Chippenham in Wiltshire, recounted how in the year 1633 the local curate was tormented by fairies, whom he had come upon dancing in a circle on the Downs. They were singing, humming, and making all sorts of strange noises. Some unearthly power kept him rooted to the spot, until the fairies caught sight of him and he fell to the ground, where they pinched him and crooned over him until he became unconscious, remaining on the grass until morning.

Seventeenth-century visitors to the fairies, such as Aubrey's curate, tended to report fairy speech as being indistinct and incomprehensible, in contrast to earlier accounts (such as that of Thomas the Rhymer), in which they were understood. Difficulty in understanding fairies is caused by our conscious, rational minds getting in the way, for many fairies speak wordlessly, straight to the heart and soul. Others use the language of the land to which they are attached, for it is deep in their being.

When you wander in the wild places of Nature, always keep your ears open for the enchanting music of the fairies, and you will catch it on the breeze.

Fairy Festivals

Fairy festivals take place at crossover points in the seasons. Equinoxes and solstices are determined by the position of the Sun, but the other four festivals are celebrated when the time feels right, so the dates given below are approximate.

There are other festivals too, such as Christmas Eve, Christmas Day, and New Year's Day. Any human festival that touches on old traditions, from Ramadan to a Japanese Flower Festival, is a fairy feast. If you celebrate these festivals and make the effort to tune into what concerns the fairies, you will draw closer to their world. If you celebrate a special meal, remember to leave a little outside afterward for the fairies.

IMBOLC

February 2 in the Northern Hemisphere
July 31 in the Southern Hemisphere

Imbolc means "in the belly," and this is the time when life stirs in the belly of the earth. Frost sparkles and the pale light lingers each evening, bringing the message that spring is on the horizon. Imbolc is the delicate crossover point from winter's depths into the New Year. It is a feast of lightness and

writing poetry. Ask the fairies to lend you a little of their magic by leaving them an offering, such as a piece of wool or a verse written just for them.

This feast is also called Candlemas, sacred to St. Bridget, who was the successor to the pagan goddess Bride (pronounced "Breed"). Bride was the keeper of the sacred flame, which represents eternal life. She is the patroness of poetry, smithcraft, childbirth, and healing, and is a very powerful fairy indeed. Invite her into your home by lighting as many candles as you like, in your windows and around your house. Ask her to bless all your projects for the coming year, and pledge a special act of caring for the natural world in return, to seal your pact as the year waxes.

brightness, but also a time of cleansing, to make way for the new. The Hag, who is Dark Goddess or Dark Fairy, gives way now to the Maiden, who is young and radiant.

Fairies love neatness and good housekeeping, so it is a good idea to have a late-winter sort-out, in preparation for fresh activity. While the fairies are busy coaxing snowdrops and crocuses out of the winter-hard earth, do something creative of your own, such as knitting, painting, or

SPRING EQUINOX

March 21 in the Northern Hemisphere
September 21 in the Southern Hemisphere

The fairies are very busy at the Spring Equinox, looking after all the flowers that are newly blooming. Scandinavian fairies become active now; the Russian cellar fairy, the Domoviyr, casts off its skin and grows a lighter one for summer; and the Russian Rusalki, or river fairies, are glimpsed by lakes swollen with melting snow.

A tree-planting project is a very fairy-friendly activity at this time. A seasonal blitz on the garden is also called for. While you are hard at work, digging and pulling away at dead winter twigs, it is easy to go into a kind of trance. This, coupled with the spell of the natural world around you, can create the perfect state of mind to catch a glimpse of fairies. You can be sure they are near you, helping you with their energies. Plant some seeds of your choice and, as you put them in the earth, close your eyes and make a special request for fairy help. Visualize the fairies tending your seeds, giving them their love and care. Ask out loud

for the fairies to help you, and sing or hum as you plant. Touch the soft soil with your bare hands and make real contact with the earth.

Place water in a pottery or glass jug (plastic or metal is best avoided) and leave it out in the noon sunshine. Ask the fairies to bless it. Imagine them dancing around it and coming up to touch it with their glimmering fingers. Use the water to give your houseplants a special spring blessing.

The Green Man is a powerful nature spirit that has been sensed by many people. He is represented in numerous churches as the Foliate Mask (a face made up of leaves), and one theory about his presence is that the masons who fabricated him had hidden sympathies with the old nature-worship. He is making his appearance now on some new park benches and monuments. However, you can make contact with the real Green Man out alone walking through woodland. Ancient and wise, he is watching you. Catch a glimpse of him behind tree trunks or in the lacework of budding branches. Hear his footfalls behind you as you walk. He is the very breath of Nature, and his strength is bursting forth in springtime.

BELTANE

April 30 in the Northern Hemisphere
October 31 in the Southern Hemisphere

Of all the festivals, Beltane is the most flagrantly joyful and sensuous, as Nature is bursting forth with beauty and excitement. This was the Celtic beginning of summer, and also marked an important transition for the people of Fairy, for it was the time when the Milesian Celts landed on the shores of south-west Ireland. With this, the last of the magical peoples, the Tuatha de Danann, receded from the world of humans into the Hollow Hills and became the people of the Sidhe. However, they and the other fairy folk have not gone very far. You will find them dancing in a bluebell wood or skipping in the sunshine, sheltered by a greening hedge. Beltane is the time when good fairies reign supreme and bad fairies retreat. Fairies are very active now and may try to steal butter, or some of the ritual fire that used to be ignited on hilltops and is still lit by modern pagans.

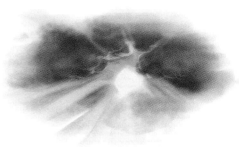

This is the maypole season, but instead you can always dance around a friendly tree. Link hands with friends, and you may find yourselves spontaneously re-creating the kind of things people used to do when seeing fairies was commonplace: lingering, walking, and talking in the open air, away from television, computers, and other modern distractions.

There are many tales of beautiful fairies marrying mortals. Such tales usually end in tragedy, for fairy and human can never truly be joined. Better to borrow some of the fairy enchantment by performing a little magic of your own! Rise early on May Day and wash your face in the dew or simply walk in it. As the rhyme says:

The fair maid who, the first of May
Goes to the fields at break of day
And walks in dew from the hawthorn tree
Will ever handsome be.

Welsh legend tells how the hero
Pwll saw the Lady Rhiannon riding
past him at Beltane and, after
pursuing her, he eventually won her.
Rhiannon is one aspect of the Fairy
Queen, riding on her white horse
between the worlds. As you sit quietly
outside, on a bank in the late spring
dusk, listen for the sound of her horse's
hooves, and open your eyes to the
shimmer of her sea-blue cloak. When
Rhiannon touches your heart, she will
fill it with love and inspiration.

MIDSUMMER

June 22 in the Northern Hemisphere
December 22 in the Southern Hemisphere

This is one of the most magical times of the year, when fairies are very active and visible, playing pranks and even, it is said, stealing away the young and beautiful to join them in the Hollow Hills. The sun is now at the height of its strength and this is an important crossover point, such as the fairies love. For at the Midsummer Solstice the sun stands still, before beginning to recede as we move into the waning half of the year.

Flowers are colorful and luxuriant, and one radiant day seems to merge into another, as late dusk meets early dawn. At no time is the natural world more inviting. Take part in it by going on quests—long walks to sacred spots, even camping out with the minimum of equipment, to draw close to the mystery that is all around, and to the Fair Folk in particular.

The rose is possibly the most sensuous bloom of all, and at midsummer it is often at its most gorgeous.

Roses in the garden are especially likely to attract fairies. Distil water from rose petals and add it to your bath, asking the fairies to lend you some of their enchantment and to help you attract love. Brew a tea from rosebuds and drink it, to increase your psychic powers. Plant a rose bush with a friend, to affirm the loving bond between you and invite the fairies into your life.

St. John's wort is a herb known to break any negative fairy enchantment and drive away depression. Pluck some on Midsummer's Day and carry it, to keep cheerful. If you wish to become pregnant, do this while walking naked in a vegetable garden!

Look out for water nymphs by streams, or for undines (or water elementals, see page 104) on the seashore—or for even the Lady of the Lake herself, rising from the luminous depths. In olden times, these beings were said to have no souls. It is closer to the truth to say that they do not have human morals. Conventions often conceal our feelings, but the beauty of the water fairies opens us to our unconscious tides; see them and let yourself be transformed.

LAMMAS

July 31 in the Northern Hemisphere
February 2 in the Southern Hemisphere

Lammas is "Loaf Mass," a Christian version of a much older festival known as Lughnasadh, or the "Feast of Lugh." Lugh was a Celtic god, lord of the Tuatha de Danann, and his name means "bright one." Lughnasadh is a major fairy festival, and many fairies become active during this period, such as the Russian Polevik, who kicks sleepy harvesters awake. It is also a time when fairies move about in preparation for winter, and processions of them may be seen as a line of twinkling lights moving between the hills in the countryside.

At Lammas, the fields are golden with corn and splashed with red poppies. It is a hazy, lazy time of holidays and abundance, but there is an underlying theme of death, for the Corn Spirit must be sacrificed in order to reap the harvest. If you walk out into a field of ripe wheat, you may sense the anger of the nature spirits at what is to be taken from the earth, even though that is part of the natural cycle of life. Gather up some ears of wheat and tie them into a bunch with red thread, to make a charm for the coming winter to hang over your hearth. At the same time, pledge an act of caring for the earth, such as clearing a derelict site in your neighborhood or garden, or planting and tending a herb, as payment for what you—and all of us—take from it.

At home, bake your own bread, using the rising of the dough as a spell to ensure that everything prospers in your life. While you are kneading the bread dough, say to yourself, "As this dough swells, so may my fortunes increase." Ask for your own personal Brownie, or house fairy, to come and help your bread rise—and remember to leave some breadcrumbs outside afterward, for the fairies.

Some say that Lugh is lord of the waning year, and his dance—through the waving, whispering corn—is a dance of death. If so, it is a reminder that all things come in cycles, and that everything is united in love and beauty. Stand at the edge of a sun-kissed wheat field and see the shimmer and sway that betrays the presence of Lugh. Take a few moments to feel respect for the earth in your heart, and understand the meaning of the Wheel of Life.

AUTUMN EQUINOX

September 21 in the Northern Hemisphere
March 21 in the Southern Hemisphere

At the Autumn Equinox, Nature stands poised between light and dark, but darkness is gaining. The veil between this world and the Otherworld is at its thinnest, and all manner of spirit visitations are more frequent now.

The hedgerows are beaded with berries, and mist lingers in the hollows. Sometimes the wind whistles in from nowhere and tosses baring branches. On other days, the mellow sun caresses the fields with slanting fingers. It is a time for reflection, but also for industry. In days gone by, preserves would be made for winter store and the help of the Good Folk would be sought by country people.

Absorb the atmosphere of the season by going blackberrying. In Celtic countries, there may be a taboo on eating blackberries, because these belong especially to fairies. However, as long as you gather them with respect

and do not denude the bramble bushes, they will hardly object. Better still, leave out some of your homemade blackberry pie or wine for them, so that they will bless you. When this month ends, leave the blackberries alone and move on. Also look out for a bramble bush that forms an arch—so much the better if it faces east/west, for that mirrors the passage of the sun. Crawl through this three times on a sunny day to be healed of physical ills, especially rheumatism and skin troubles.

At this mysterious time, pay honor to Queen Mab. Her special gift is to bring dreams and visions to birth within us. She is really one of many manifestations of the Goddess, in her autumnal guise of wise-woman and Lady of Magic, and she is linked with ancient ideas of sovereignty—for the king drew his power from the land, and Mab presided.

Preferably at the Full Moon closest to the equinox, place good-quality wine in a stemmed glass or chalice, and take it into the garden or a secluded place.

Raise the glass to the Moon, say, "Mab, I honor you" and pour some of the wine onto the earth. Drink a little and say, "Mab, I drink with you." Then return home, light a bright-green candle beside your bed, gaze at the flame and say, "Mab, give me wisdom." Place some jasmine or rose oil on your pillow, extinguish the candle—and drift into Fairyland. This is a little ritual that you can repeat during any Full Moon if you wish.

SAMHAIN

October 31 in the Northern Hemisphere
April 30 in the Southern Hemisphere

Samhain means "summer's end" and is pronounced "sa-wen." This ancient Celtic festival at the official start of winter was later Christianized as Halloween—a time when the dead were remembered. There was always a sinister aspect to Samhain, because certain sacrifices had to be made in order to survive the coming cold weather. Animals had to be slaughtered, and some say that human sacrifice took place to propitiate the spirits. Sacrifice, however, is a corruption of nature worship, for life is hard enough as it is and all we have to do is show respect.

Barrow mounds, shrouded in mist, are particularly eerie places at Samhain. Draw close, if you dare, and sit quietly. Do you hear the strange, far-off noise of fairy music, or the sound of knocking? Maybe the mound will open for you and unearthly light will stream over the barren fields. After Samhain, the earth is given over to the powers of darkness and decay. No crops or berries may be harvested

after this time,
because the Phooka,
a malevolent Irish
fairy, blights them. The
true meaning here, of course,
is that death and decay have a place in
the natural order, requiring due honor
and respect lest they get out of hand.

Traditionally, this is the start of the
story-telling season. While the wind
whistles around the eaves or the mist
comes down outside, gather family
or friends around your hearth—
preferably with a real fire burning in
it. If you do not have an open hearth,
substitute a collection of large, burning
candles. Sit round and speak of times
gone by and people who have passed
over to the other side. Ask the Beloved
Dead to be present, if you wish (but
note that this is *not* a seance, and the
Beloved Dead are *invited*, not
summoned). Laugh, share funny
stories, feast, and drink.

Cerridwen is the Underworld
goddess and the Fairy Hag most
associated with this time. In her magic
cauldron, she stirs a brew that confers
inspiration and transformation.
Simmer up a hearty soup of root
vegetables or pumpkin, to share with
friends, then light a black candle and
ask Cerridwen to guide you through
the darkness into the light. You will
be both safe and wise.

YULE

December 22 in the Northern Hemisphere
June 22 in the Southern Hemisphere

Yule is the Midwinter Solstice, when
the sun again appears to stand still,
as it did at midsummer, but the season
is poised for the return of light.
Celebrations of Christ's birth were
moved to coincide with the much
more ancient solstice.

As you deck your Christmas tree,
remember that the evergreen is a
powerful symbol of the enduring life in
Nature. Of course, it has a fairy on top
of it, confirming that it is a festival of
the Fair Folk, who also rejoice in the
sun's rebirth. Decorating your tree is an
important magical act, for the
decorations are fairy charms. Each
member of the family should hang at
least one special charm of their own,
to enable a wish to come true.

Jack Frost is an active fairy in the
cold weather, painting windows with
intricate lacework. In Russia he is
called Father Frost, the soul of winter,
covering the trees in ice. Do not shrink

from the frost fairy—go out and
wonder at his works and he will
reward you with hope and joy, just as
in Russia Father Frost brings presents
for the children on New Year's Day.

By far the best-known and most
powerful fairy at Yule is Father

Christmas himself. Today we know him by his robes of red and white, but in the past he also wore green and other colors. As we have seen, red is the color both of life and death, and many fairies wear red caps. The hearty red of Father Christmas is a sign that he is an Otherworld being—very much alive, but not of this earth. He is recognized all over the world, as Kris Kringle in Germany and Père Noël in France. In Brazil he is Papa Noël, and in China Dun Che Loa. He is the essence of

Yuletide mystery, joy, and renewal, and, like many traditional fairies, he comes in and out via the hearth.

When all is quiet on Christmas Eve, get ready to welcome Father Christmas—light a candle and look at the stars. Pledge a gift for a friend and one for the world, and ask for a special gift to answer your heart's desire. Write your wish on a piece of paper and "post" it up the chimney if you have an open fire. If not, burn it in the candle flame. Can you hear those sleigh bells?

Fairy Trees

Many fairies are linked to just one tree or plant, or to a group of trees. Trees are extremely special—a fact recognized by the Native Americans, who call them "The Standing People." Often you will come upon a tree and be very aware of its spirit, which is usually warm, wise, and welcoming; it can be very healing to be close to such trees. Occasionally, however, a tree may be not so well disposed towards humans (as the hobbits found in The Lord of the Rings with Old Man Willow), and then it is best to keep your distance.

In times gone by, the earth was covered in forest, and when we go deep into woodland, we really are in the presence of beings that are unutterably ancient, for all the accumulated wisdom of the ages is embodied in each tree. The primeval forest is also a metaphor for our unconscious, our deepest and most primitive impulses and yearnings. Tree fairies can teach us a great deal about ourselves, if we have the courage to listen. When we are alone in Nature,

we are able to hear our own thoughts and feelings more clearly, and it is easier to be truthful with ourselves. Long ago, many trees were considered to be the home of oracles, with the deity whispering through the leaves.

THE FAIRY TRIAD

Oak, ash, and thorn are termed the Fairy Triad, and where these three grow, fairies can easily be seen. Many fairies are reputed to live in the majestic oak, and to fell one is to risk the wrath of the Old Gods—namely, fairies. Druid worship took place in groves, and the oak grove was especially sacred. Ash may be used to protect against fairies, when carried as a staff or wand, but also offers a potential gateway between the worlds, as it was the tree upon which the Norse god Odin hung, to gain the secret of the runes. The twisted shape of hawthorn is magical indeed, especially when growing near a barrow mound or in groups of three. It is courting disaster to damage such a tree, and even dozing beneath one may be to risk fairy displeasure. Like much of nature, trees have been abused. Always proceed with respect for trees in order to retain the goodwill of the Fair Folk.

Fairy Flowers and Plants

Every plant is in essence a "fairy" plant, because fairies take care of them. However, there are some plants that are especially notable. Many flowers are linked to fairies, and in the Balkans, fairies are said to be born in flowers, to tend them as they bloom and fade.

The idea of flower fairies was popularized by Cicely Mary Barker (1895–1973), who illustrated the immensely successful Flower Fairy series of books, in which a fairy is depicted for each bloom, wearing clothes that look like the flower itself. This may appear to be a pretty fiction, but (like so many works of the imagination) it draws its inspiration from the subtle realms—for each flower does have a fairy and, when this is revealed to us, has some of the characteristics of the plant.

The wild rose, primrose, bluebell, cowslip, marigold, foxglove, and red campion are among many flowers especially associated with fairies. Herbs are a fairy favorite because they are both beautiful (generally) and useful. Wearing thyme can enable you to see fairies. Nettles and gorse are said to deter fairies—except, of course, for the Nettle and Gorse Fairies themselves. Fairies are said to live inside stalks of straw, which can be twisted to form an amulet. A four-leafed clover is especially lucky, so if you find such a leaf, treasure it. And, seven grains of wheat laid on a four-leafed clover enable you to see fairies.

FAIRY MUSHROOMS

One plant especially associated with fairies is the fly agaric (*Amanita muscaria*), a red and white spotted mushroom. Fairies are often depicted sitting on this mushroom, and the red caps worn by many fairies may be linked to this plant. Fly agaric is psychotropic (that is, it can affect the mind, emotions or behavior) and was ingested by European shamans to induce visions. Many of the reported visits to Fairyland—with their enhanced colors, strange music, and time distortion—sound like drug-induced "trips." So might the whole idea of fairies arise from drug use? Or is it more likely that the essence of certain plants, when used correctly, can take us into the true world of vibrant, enchanted Nature? Of course, to experiment with this would be dangerous in the extreme, but experienced shamans from Native American and other traditions have been using such plants since time immemorial. More than chemistry is at work here—the very soul of the plant combines with that of the human being and reveals a magical world to the traveler: the world of Fairyland.

Fairy Animals

In ancient times, animals were believed to be the teachers, guardians, and soul companions of humanity. In shamanic traditions, an animal can be a totem or a unifying emblem, or it can be a "power animal," acting as a kind of "hotline" to a certain kind of energy. Animals are close to Nature and are generally honest and true to themselves. Small wonder that many animals are beloved of the fairies, and that numerous fairies assume their shape from time to time.

Witches' "familiars" are a potent connection to the spirit world. A favorite "familiar" is the cat, which has close links with fairies and may indeed be a shape-shifted fairy, according to Irish and European folklore. Tailless Manx cats were fairy-bred, and the Fairy Cat-King dwells as an ordinary cat by day, but goes on royal procession by night to wreak vengeance on any who have injured him. In times of persecution, cats often suffered with their owners. Who can blame the Cat-King?

CLOVEN-HOOFED ANIMALS

Fairies have a special affinity with cows, possibly because these creatures give generously of their milk and are closely associated with the Mother Goddess. Fairies were blamed for stealing milk from cows, either from a distance or by appearing as a hedgehog or a hare and suckling. Fairies who do this are drawing on the life force of the cow, rather than on the actual milk. There are also tales of cows from the Otherworld with red or rounded ears,

and these may be found wandering on the seashore, having strayed from their fairy home beneath the waves. Such cows give a wonderful supply of milk.

The stag was a sacred animal to the Celts. It is one of the forms of the Horned God, who embodies the mystical link between hunter and hunted, and both protects and culls the wild creatures of the forest. The Horned God was debased as the Devil, when the old pagan gods were demonized by Christianity. However, he has nothing at all to do with anything demonic and is more properly regarded as the Fairy King in one of his most awesome guises. Fairy women often take on the shape of a red deer, and fairies in general do not like hunters and may throw elf-shot at them—usually in the form of small flint arrow-heads.

Fairies also turn into goats, or have goats' legs and hooves. The Greek nature god Pan was half-man, half-goat, to show that we all have animal instincts and knowledge within us. Pan

(and, along with him, the goat) has also been demonized, and in English folklore there exists the belief that a goat cannot be visible for an entire 24 hours, for it must go to pay homage to the Devil—or the fairies.

HORSES AND DOGS

Horses are believed to be able to gallop between the worlds, carrying the rider to Fairyland. Fairies love these subtle, graceful creatures. The people of the Sidhe keep magical horses within the Hollow Hills, made of flame and swift as the wind. Scottish water fairies or Kelpies often appear as gray horses, and these are evil beings who may tempt a traveler onto their back, only to ride them swiftly to their death in a watery grave.

Fairy dogs guide humans into the Underworld, and may be either friendly or malevolent. There have been numerous stories of black dogs haunting areas of Britain, and boding ill. In fact, "Black Dog" may be a metaphor for depression, showing an unconscious recognition of the power of such apparitions. Other fairy dogs appear to be white or green and have red ears. Many legends tell of a pack of spectral hounds that hunt the souls of the dead in the Wild Hunt (see below and page 91).

BIRDS

Many birds are associated with fairies. The cuckoo is the herald of spring, going back into the fairy mounds during winter. Owls are associated with darker fairies, such as Gwyn ap Nudd, lord of the Underworld, who rides out in the Wild Hunt to herd souls into his kingdom. Ravens guard fairy treasure, and the death goddess, the Morrigan, appeared as one. Fairies and enchanted humans both take on the form of swans, and the little wren is a fairy bird.

FROGS

Fairies could also take on the shape of frogs, and there are many stories of humans having been turned into frogs as punishment for committing various transgressions. Fairies who guard wells may be seen as frogs, and frogs were sacred to the Celts, who connected them with healing.

You do not have to kiss a frog in order to receive a blessing from the fairies. Just show them that you respect and love the natural world in all its amazing manifestations (even the apparently ugly ones), and the fairies will reward you.

Time in Fairyland

In the realm of the fairies, time passes differently because they inhabit another dimension, with laws and measurements that are different from our own. People who enter Fairyland usually believe that they have been there only a short while, but when they come back all that was familiar has long ago passed away, and no one remembers them any more. Conversely, sometimes it may seem that days or years have been spent with the Fair Folk, yet it later transpires that the traveler has been gone only a few moments.

One tale is told of a young Welshman from Pembrokeshire who spotted a fairy ring while tending sheep on a hillside. Against all warnings, he entered the ring to dance with the fairies. Instantly, he found himself in the Otherworld, where there was so much splendor and beauty that all thoughts of returning left him, and he spent many joyful years feasting and dancing with the fairies. While he was there, he was warned not to drink from a certain fountain, but the thought of doing so played on his mind until eventually he plunged into the forbidden waters. Immediately, he found himself back with his sheep, just as he had left them—only a few minutes of mortal time having elapsed.

THE LEGEND OF OISIN

The story of Oisin, from Irish legend, is very different, and is partly a metaphor for what happens when humans cease to believe in the magical, and in the power of Nature. Oisin was the son of

the mighty Fion mac Cumhail (pronounced "Finn McCool"), leader of the Fianna warriors, and the deer goddess Sadb (pronounced "Sa-eve"). While he was out one day hunting in the forest, the beautiful fairy Niamh of the Golden Hair, daughter of the sea god Manannan, came up to him. She had chosen him as her lover, and she begged him to come away to Tir-nan-Og, Land of Eternal Youth across the Western Seas. For 300 years they lived together in happiness, but then Oisin wished to see his home once more. Niamh gave him a magical horse for the journey, warning him not to let his feet touch the earth. When Oisin came back to Ireland, he was saddened to see that everyone had been converted to Christianity, and the men had less strength. He saw three men struggling to shift a rock and leant over to help them. As he did so, his saddle-girth slipped and he fell to the ground. In an

instant he became decrepit and blind, and his fairy horse vanished. St. Patrick came upon him and tried to convert him to Christianity, but Oisin could see no attraction in an Afterlife without feasting and beautiful women, so he remained pagan.

In this story, the pagan world-view and the Christian come up against each other, with the former shown as vibrant and powerful, but depotentized in the face of lack of reverence for the earth and the Fair Folk. Oisin's sudden aging also suggests that Tir-nan-Og is the Land of the Dead, and that contact with the earth brings back the reality of mortality. Thus too with many travelers to Fairyland, whose bodies crumbled to dust on their return, suggesting that they were truly dead.

is a rare example of a mortal–fairy union with a happy ending.

TIME CROSSOVERS

The pace of time within this world and Fairyland may differ in a variety of ways, but nonetheless the worlds seem to interlock. Dancers in fairy circles tend to be rescued after a year or a year and a day, while a month in Fairyland may equal a hundred years in the human world or an hour may equate to a day, or vice versa. The seasons are very important, as we have already seen (see page 62), and at transitional times in the seasonal round, the entrance to Fairyland may be open. Certain times of the day are also significant—namely, dawn, dusk, midday, and midnight.

Time is something we struggle to understand in the ordinary world. It has a mysterious quality and may appear to move either fast or slow. Perhaps time itself is an illusion created by our mortality, from which the fairies can free us, now and again.

Similar tales to that of Oisin are to be found worldwide, even in Japan. An Italian version tells how the hero marries the fairy maiden Fortune, and when he asks to return to his home, she goes with him, thereby preventing him making the mistakes of Oisin. On finding that his mother is long dead, he returns with Fortune to Fairyland, where they live happily ever after. This

Fairy Processions, Travel, and Transport

The host is rushing 'twixt night and day
And where is there hope or deed as fair?
Caoilte tossing his burning hair,
And Niamh calling Away, come away.

W.B. YEATS, "THE HOSTING OF THE SIDHE."

The Fair Folk have a reputation for going about in magnificent cavalcade, often behind their king and queen. In Scotland, such a procession was called the Fairy Rade (that is, "ride"). Some fairies—for instance, the Tuatha de Danann—may resemble humans in build, although possessed of an ethereal, hypnotic beauty. They were believed to ride out hunting and hawking, and their horses were as beautiful as they were, white in color and with silver bells hanging from saddle and bridle. Such fairies are also known as "Heroic Fairies," for they are the more noble of the species (at least from a human perspective). These are the ancient gods and goddesses,

conceived as medieval knights and ladies (for that is how they resonate in our hearts and minds), and still alive and powerful within the land.

In his book *Irish Fairy and Folk Tales*, the poet W.B. Yeats describes two kinds of fairies, the solitary fairy and the trooping fairy. There may also be a third grouping, that of the domestic fairy. Trooping fairies come in all shapes and sizes, and may be of either good or evil intent. Usually they wear green, in contrast to the preferred red of solitary fairies. Sometimes they are very tiny, around 1–2 ft. (30–60 cm) in height, and sometimes human size or larger, like the Heroic Fairies.

Fin Bheara (also known as Finvarra) is the Fairy King of Ulster. He is also credited with being King of the Dead. One Halloween he was seen by an Irish fisherman, drawing up to a Fairy Fair in a coach with four white horses. The horses of the fairies, and their ability to ride like the wind, were well known.

One of the most eerie of fairy cavalcades is the Wild Hunt, headed by the Welsh King of the Underworld, Gwyn ap Nudd, who herds the souls of

the dead and a host of demons into the subterranean realms. Gwyn ap Nydd is said to dwell beneath Glastonbury Tor in southern England. In the 1940s, the Wild Hunt was heard not far away at Taunton at Halloween. However, there are those who report having heard and seen it in many places.

LEY LINES AND INTERFACES

Fairy processions are most likely to be seen upon fairy paths (see page 53). Such paths may be ley lines, which are believed to be lines of subtle energy running through the earth. These lines are generally straight and extend between significant markers, such as a hilltop, a megalithic site, a church (for churches were often built on old sites of pagan worship) or an ancient tree. Hauntings and apparitions of all kinds are more frequent on these lines, which may be an interface between this world and the Otherworld.

Indeed, fairy processions are often the scene for some crucial encounter between mortal and fairy, as in the Border-country "Ballad of Tamlane." Tamlane was a seductive fairy youth who haunted Carterhaugh Wood. The king's beautiful daughter Janet fell in love with him and discovered that he was a mortal taken by the fairies. To win him back, she had to seize him from the fairy cavalcade, at midnight at the crossroads, and hang onto him through a series of horrifying shape-shifting, caused by the Fairy Queen. Janet bravely carried out her mission and Tamlane was later freed to become her husband.

Irish fairies are more likely to travel by supernatural means than on splendid horses. Some travel on bundles of grass, which they ride in the same way that witches ride their brooms. Others move in the twinkling of an eye by uttering a magical word. Despite the fact that fairies are often depicted with wings, traditional fairies are rarely known to travel using them. The gauzy pinions are merely a sign that fairies can move about unrestrained by time, space, and gravity. Fairies can also levitate humans, animals, and even buildings, should the need arise.

At the start of the 19th century, near Glen Eathie, a brother and sister saw the last Fairy Rade. A cavalcade of small creatures rode past, and the boy asked them who they were and where they were going. He was told they were not of the race of Adam, and that the People of Peace would never again be seen in Scotland. With the coming of industry and the Enlightenment, it may have seemed that there was no place for fairies. However, while flowers grow and songs are sung, there will always be fairies not far away.

Fairy Gold and Gifts

Fairies have uncounted treasures in their mounds and palaces. The walls and pavements are made of silver and gold, and precious stones stud the architecture. Treasures that humans have lost, or buried and forgotten, grace their halls. When a ship is wrecked, the water fairies take the spoils, and all the minerals and jewels within the earth are theirs to begin with. Some lucky people are led by the fairies to their valuables and given wondrous gifts, and it is the fairies who lead miners to the ore. However, woe betide the human being who tries to rob the fairies of what is theirs.

D warfs are Norse earth fairies that guard all the underground riches of the Mother Goddess. Many are well disposed toward humans and will help them find utensils and crockery for weddings and christenings. Dwarfs are experts at smithcraft, fashioning intricate cloak-pins, bracelets, armbands and torques for other fairies. Robert Kirk (see page 18) described how all these were

made from the finest yellow-gold, set with jewels. The Sidhe especially love magnificent adornment, including

magical swords, very light in weight, whose hilts are set with gems. Fairy gold, however, may not be what it seems, and may turn to dust or smoke when taken into mortal realms.

ABSTRACT GIFTS

By far the greatest gifts given by the fairies, however, are those of an intangible kind. The fairies love people who are genuine, kind and truthful, and who are not pretentious or over-materialistic. They like luxury, cleanliness, and generosity, and of course they need to be treated with respect. Then the fairies may really bless a human being—possibly with beauty and riches, with general good luck, or with the love of a special person. They may save his or her life, endow them with healing abilities or a knowledge of herbs, or make them irresistible to the opposite sex. Witches often get their healing and magical powers straight from the fairies.

PRACTICAL GIFTS

Fairies have been known to give gifts of a practical kind, and one species of fairy with a history of being helpful in this way is the Cornish and Welsh Ellyll, which is a tiny elf. A story is told of a Welsh farmer called Rowli Pugh, who was renowned in the neighborhood for his bad luck. Rowli became despondent and decided to move far away. As he sat thinking sadly about his plans, a tiny man appeared in front of him. "Don't worry now, I know about your problems," said the elf. "I have ways of fixing things. Tell your wife to leave a candle burning when she goes to bed, and tell no one we have spoken." Then the elf vanished, and Rowli went home and did as he had been told. His wife swept the hearth and left things neat and clean, and from then on each night the fairies came and did her cooking and sewing, her laundry and housework. Much cheered by this, Rowli decided to stay and his farm prospered. After a while his wife grew curious, and in the dead of night she crept down and peeped at the fairies through a crack in the door. The elves were dancing and laughing as they worked and, when she saw them, the young woman could not help giggling too. The elves heard her and vanished, never to return. However, they left their good luck behind, for Rowli's farm continued to thrive.

FAIRY GODMOTHERS

Of course, the best-known bringers of fairy gifts are fairy godmothers, which feature in many fairy stories, such as *Cinderella* and *Snow White*. Fairies such as these are known in numerous lands. In Italy, the fairy godmother is called Fata, a name derived from "Fate." Befind is her name in Ireland; Disir in Scandinavia; Holda in Germany; Rozanica in Poland; Udelnicy in Russia; and she has many other names worldwide. The number three is associated with fairy godmothers, for three is a creative number (as in Mother/Father/Child). There may be three godmothers, they may appear three days after the birth and there are other variations. Fairy godmothers are invited by cleaning the house and by offering gifts such as honey or coins. They may bring many blessings, although one dubious gift is that of foretelling the fate of the child. Fairy godmothers are linked to ancient goddesses who spun the fate of humankind. They may also appear

at marriage and at death, showing that
they are linked to life's transitions.

Fairy gifts must be treated with
caution and respect. They are rarely
of this world, often they do not last
and sometimes they have a price.
They are as ephemeral and
mysterious as fairies themselves,
and enrich those most whose
grasp upon them is gentle.

Fairy Protocol

We are breaching fairy protocol on every page of this book, because fairies do not like to be called "fairies"! There are many alternative names for them, including the Fair Folk, the Good People, the Gentry, the Little Folk, the Honest Folk, the Hill People, the Good Neighbors, the Men of Peace and others.

Not so very long ago, such names were used by people who were fearful that fairies were listening to what they said, and who did not wish to arouse their resentment and mischief. In general, fairies do not like people to be curious about them, and to tell of experiences with the fairies is to incur their displeasure. Fairy blessings spoken of lightly tend to disappear.

The Fair Folk are extremely private, and one of the worst faux pas is to spy on them or boast of encounters with them. Tales of Elizabethan encounters describe how fairy gold was given, only to be snatched away again when its origin was made public.

Traditionally, those who spy on fairies risk being blinded by them. Sometimes midwives were stolen to help with fairy births, and were given ointment to place on the eyes of the infant (who was presumably part-human) so that he or she could see fairies. Should the ointment be used by the midwife, she might be struck blind by the fairies. Probably a realistic interpretation of this is that if we use psychic gifts inappropriately, we risk losing them.

Fairy lovers like to remain secret, and to speak of such trysts is to risk being "dumped." A 12th-century story tells how a knight called Sir Launval fell in love with a beautiful fairy called

Tryamour (meaning "Trial of Love"), who came to him with priceless gifts, including her own affections. When he allowed himself to be pushed into talking about her, all she had given him crumbled to dust and she no longer appeared. However, because she loved him, Tryamour eventually forgave him and returned—a rare happy ending to a human–fairy romance.

Fairies tend to believe that what humans own is theirs too. This is not as unfair as it may appear, for all we own upon the earth is, in fact, borrowed, and cannot be taken with us when we depart this life. Fairies also set great store by the truth, and even bad fairies do not tell outright lies— they simply avoid issues and tend to speak ambiguously.

FAIRY OFFERINGS

To attract the benign attention of fairies, it is best to make sure that your environment is clean and tidy. Fairies like to have a warm place left for them near the fire, and if you have an open fire (best, by far, for fairies), leave it smouldering at night so that they can enjoy it. They also like to have milk, wine or other choice beverages left for them. If you grow your own fruit or vegetables, leave the last of the produce in the ground or on the bush, as an offering to the fairies. In times gone by, when cows were milked by hand, the first few drops of milk were allowed to fall to the ground for the fairies. This makes sense in terms of Nature worship, for it means returning to Mother Earth some of her gifts, as a token of respect.

Fairies must never be given

FAIRY MORALITY

You can never be sure when a needy person is a fairy in disguise. Always be kind to beggars, look after old people and even be gentle with frogs! A fairy—in the shape of a crone or poor man—may ask for help with a broken tool, or for guidance on his or her path. Give this and you are likely to be rewarded; refuse and the consequences could be disastrous. The Disney film *Beauty and the Beast* portrays the fate of the arrogant prince who refused shelter to an old woman, who was actually a powerful fairy. She turned him into a beast until someone should love him, despite his ugliness, and show him that appearances do not tell the whole story.

There is much morality and symbolism in the behavior of fairies towards mortals (along with things that make no sense at all). This should make us humble in the face of our narrow perspectives and inadequate understanding. One of the gifts of fairies is to make us puzzle, so that our awareness grows.

clothes, for that drives them away. And it is important not to say "thank you" to the fairies for their gifts, because that makes them angry. Do not give back to them more than they have given (or lent) you, for they find that insulting. The basis for all this is that we must not assume fairies have our own petty human standards.

Water Fairies

The Element of Water

To the ancients, the entire earth was made from four basic Elements: Earth, Fire, Air, and Water. These Elements are described on pages 46–47, where they are connected to the four fairy citadels.

We can think of the Elements as having their own compartments or levels within the spirit world, but of course they also exist within our world, carrying with them certain subtle and symbolic properties, as well as the physical properties we know so well. Many fairies have an affinity with a particular Element, but in addition occultists believe that certain spirits, called "elementals," specifically express the energy of their own associated Element in nature.

The generic name for water elementals is "undines." (This is also the name for an individual water sprite, called Undine, whose story is told on pages 112–113.) Undines are the pure manifestation of the spirit of water, while other water fairies may be thought of as having more of a liking for water, with a differentiated personality of their own, their own habits, gifts, stories, and traditions.

Water fairies are possibly the most numerous of all spirits. This is partly because it may be easier for fairies to manifest where the air is damp. Water has many mysterious properties and may retain impressions and images, as described by the Cambridge don T.C. Lethbridge in his book *Ghost and Ghoul*, published in 1961. Some people may look upon this as being a matter for fringe science and psychology, but those who are aware of the fairy kingdom realize that where there is water, so too there may be a window between the worlds.

Water is associated with the emotions, with unconscious longings and repressed fears. This is reflected in the appearance of water fairies, who are often very seductive and captivatingly beautiful. Possibly because men tend to be less in touch with their emotions than women, the water fairy generally manifests as an exquisite female, while water sprites are risky, because the realm of emotions is threatening to the rational, conscious mind.

But what of the arid daytime world that our rationality has created and that we unquestioningly inhabit? Is it a fulfilling and meaningful environment? Or do we thirst for something more mystical and intriguing? Perhaps it is worth taking the plunge and following the mer-people into their shimmering, watery abode.

The Selkie

Once upon a time, in the cold northern lands, a weary hunter was returning home, late at night. His journey took him close to the seashore, where the full moon bathed the waters and the sands shone white as pearl. He pushed through the bushes and then, to his amazement, saw three beautiful women dancing naked, where the waves rippled about their slender feet.

Mesmerized, the hunter watched, and it seemed to him that eerie music played in the light sea-breeze. He looked down, and there on the sands lay three seal-skins, one for each of the graceful dancers. The hunter had heard tales of seal-women, whose soulful eyes betrayed the fact that they had human souls. He was lonely, and longed for a wife to share his nights. He looked again at the lovely dancers and, on impulse, seized one of the skins and buttoned it up inside his jerkin.

The dance was ending. With silvery laughter the women skipped over to retrieve their skins, slipping inside them and diving into the waves. Only one, the most beautiful of all, could not find her skin and was looking for it in increasing panic as the hunter confronted her.

"I have your skin," he told her. "Come with me and marry me. I will give you back your skin after seven years, and you may do as you please." Secretly, the hunter believed that the seal-woman would be so happy with him that she would give up all thoughts of the cold ocean in favor of the warmth of his hearth. How little he understood the call of the waves and their haunting music.

What could the poor seal-maiden do? She consented and went away with the hunter, and they lived together happily enough. She did all that was expected of her. Only her huge, gray eyes were distant, gazing every so often toward the sea. She bore the hunter a son and loved him dearly, but her skin grew dry and cracked, and her beautiful face was sad. At the end of seven years she came to her husband and begged for her seal-skin, but he became angry. "Would you leave your son?" he challenged her. "Would you go and disappear into the waves?"

The seal-woman became even quieter and more sorrowful, and her eyes became larger and larger, like great pools. Yet never did she shed a tear, for some sorrows are too great for crying. Her son loved her dearly and did all he could to cheer her up. He listened to his parents talking and realized the truth about his mother. Unable to bear the thought of her unhappiness, he took to following his father around stealthily, until one day he saw him dig up a seal-skin, check that it was intact and inter it again.

The boy was overjoyed. Now he could make his mother smile. He waited until his father was out hunting and returned to where the skin was buried. Swiftly, he dug it up and ran with it to his mother. How her gray eyes shone when she saw her skin. Hardly stopping to embrace the boy, she ran toward the shore, where she slipped into the skin and made for the waters. The boy ran after her, crying, "Mother, don't leave me—please take me with you!" For an instant the seal-woman hesitated. Then she caught hold of the boy, breathed her magic breath into him and carried him with her, beneath the waves.

In the underwater world, the boy learnt many wondrous things, absorbing the wisdom and grace of his mother's people. But he knew he could not stay for ever, for his destiny lay in the earthly world, with his father. When the time was right, his mother took him back to the shore and, kissing him for the last time, took sorrowful leave of him.

The devastated hunter was overjoyed to see his boy back again, and helped him to adapt once more to life on land. But every time the lad looked out at the moonlit strand, he could feel the presence of his mother. At length he became a renowned musician, and his greatest pleasure was to sit upon the beach and play, while the seal-people cavorted far out on the waves.

WHAT THE STORY MEANS

The story of the Selkie comes from the Scottish islands of Orkney and Shetland. There are several versions, which vary slightly, but they all have the same theme. The hauntingly beautiful Selkies were known to mate occasionally with humans and to awaken in them a yearning for the Otherworld. Inevitably, the union ended in tragedy, for the Selkie must

return to her watery home and, if trapped, eventually escaped, just as water runs from between the fingers of a cupped hand.

The story shows that the greatest gift arising from a mating between human and fairy is creative inspiration. It is a mistake to try to control and imprison the elusive magic of the fairy, for that is to destroy the very thing one loves—and it is courting disaster to break a promise, as the hunter-husband did. However, in the son of the huntsman and the Selkie, the fairies' gifts are realized, for he is able to play the most enchanting music, which is one of the ways we have of bridging the gap between this world and the Otherworld.

The sea represents emotions, but these are not just personal emotions and ordinary human bonds. The sea signifies the longings of humanity—all the memories and feelings of the ages that are too overwhelming, too deep ever to be cast aside by a being as sensitive as the Selkie. She belongs to the collective emotional pool, and she must dance the dance of Life—she has far more to experience than simply the domestic joys of marriage and motherhood. For us,

the Selkie represents the longing of the soul for its true home, which may be very distant and different from our everyday home. The Selkie teaches us to listen to the deepest songs of our heart and to follow its yearnings, for only in that way can we find peace.

The message of the Selkie is there for you—in the gray and green, the purple and wine of the northern ocean, as it swirls around pewter rocks and ripples out to meet the misty horizon. Hear the call of your heart, but first understand that you must be honest with yourself. If you are keeping up appearances in order to feel secure and accepted, you may be paying too heavy a price. Don your seal-skin and have the courage to plunge into the waves.

The Undine

"Undine" means wave, and undines are the sea fairies of ancient Greece, who appeared in the Aegean Sea as seahorses with human faces. More usually they have the appearance of a beautiful human, but they lack souls. The idea of a "soul" in Christian tradition is tied in with damnation and salvation—that undines have no soul means that they are outside human laws.

A story is told of a handsome knight called Huldebrand, who fell in love with Undine, whom he met in an enchanted wood. He took her home as his bride, but water sprang everywhere from beneath her slender feet, and folk began to whisper that she was not human. Huldebrand turned to his old sweetheart Bertalda, whom the other water fairies began to torment. Undine trapped the fairies in a well, and Huldebrand took her back. However, to pay for a trinket that the fairies had stolen from Bertalda, Undine pulled a coral necklace from the Danube for her. Seeing this, her husband accused her of still being a fairy and not fit to be with humans, whereupon Undine sadly disappeared beneath the waves. He and Bertalda planned to marry, but on their wedding morning Huldebrand was seen embracing a misty form near the waterside, whereupon he fell dead.

In this, as in many stories, union with a water fairy proves fatal to a human. There are several meanings to this. It is true that contact with fairies can be "fatal" (or nearly so) to the modern, rationalist outlook, for the world of enchantment does not operate by logic. This would appear to be most dangerous to men, who are presumably most tempted by the magical because it is opposite to their usual way of thinking and being. However, folktales also reflect a Christianity-induced fear of what were really the old goddesses and gods of Nature. The undines are often prepared to meet us halfway, but we must accept that their fluid world, where images dissolve in a watery prism and nothing is as it seems, is as valid as ours. We must let it teach us about beauty and mystery, and never expect to understand it. Paradoxically, in this way we may come to know it, deep in our souls.

Ningyo

Ningyo is a Japanese water fairy who cries
pearls instead of tears. Some say that Ningyo has
the head of a human and the body of a fish. Others believe it
is clad in sheer silk robes that move about it, like waves. Ningyos
dwell in gorgeous palaces beneath the sea, and are very seductive.

Urashima Taro was a young fisherman with a kindly nature. One day, while returning home, he came upon some youths tormenting a turtle. When he could not make them stop, he offered to buy the creature from them. The youths grabbed his money and ran, so the fisherman placed the poor turtle in the shallows and watched as it recovered and swam away. Out in his boat next day, Urashima heard someone calling his name. Looking down, he saw the turtle he had rescued, and was amazed when it invited him to visit the King's Palace beneath the waves. Urashima climbed on its back and the turtle grew much larger, taking him down to a magnificent palace. Brilliant fish ushered him into the presence of a lovely Sea Princess, who told Urashima that she was, in fact, the turtle he had rescued. The fisherman was utterly smitten, and he and the maiden lived in bliss for three days. Urashima then became worried about his parents and insisted on visiting them. His lady gave him a small box as a talisman, with instructions not to open it. Urashima promised to obey. On returning to his village, he was dismayed, for everything was different, and folk told of a young fisherman who had disappeared 300 years ago. With nothing left of his home, Urashima could only return to the underwater palace, but first he rested on the shore in bewilderment. Seeking some answers, he pulled out the talisman box and opened it. A violet mist rose from it and enveloped him, whereupon he crumbled to dust.

This tale warns us—as so many do—that time passes differently in Fairyland, and that if we forget our world, we may not get back to it. It warns of too great an immersion in fairy matters, but also, in a sense, of too *little*. It was Urashima's lack of faith and questing human mind that killed him. Our error is to try to have our cake and eat it, too!

The Gwargedd Annwn

The Gwargedd Annwn (pronounced "grageth anoon") is a Welsh
water sprite, usually female, blonde, and slender. Because of their
beauty, these sprites are irresistible to men, yet they can be devoted
wives—if their mortal spouses deserve them.

A Welsh tale recounts how a farmer spied a wondrous maid, combing her hair in a mountain pool. He offered her his bread, but she said it was too hard, and disappeared below the waves. The next day his mother gave him soft dough, which the maiden again refused. On the third day she accepted a lightly baked loaf. Her father, the Lord of the Lake, said she could marry the farmer, with a sizeable dowry, but that he would lose all if he struck his wife three times. The couple married and lived very happily. The fairy was a good wife and bore him three sons, but her behavior was odd, for she would cry at happy times such as the harvest, and laugh at funerals. A couple of times her husband gave her a hard nudge, and when he did it a third time, she accused him of striking her three times and left for the bottom of the lake, with all the animals from her dowry. However, she frequently visited her sons, teaching them the secrets of herbal medicine, for the Gwargedd Annwn is a great gift to humanity.

The Lady of the Lake, of Arthurian legend, was a Gwargedd Annwn. She stole the baby Lancelot from his human mother and brought him up as her own in the underwater realm, lovingly preparing him for his heroic future. She endowed Arthur with his magical sword, Excalibur, whose sheath guarded the wearer from harm. She has also been called Vivienne, Nimue, and Niniane.

Totally benign and generous, the Gwargedd Annwn offers all the blessings of fairy magic to humankind. Sadly, human beings all too often fail to understand fairy values and wisdom, and are not able to make proper use of the gifts laid before them. These water sprites continue to hope that we will be able to join them in their world of enchantment and light. Our task is to keep practicing.

The Mermaid

Mermaids are well known from folklore and art as maidens with the upper body of a beautiful woman and the lower body of a fish, although Scottish tales say they have legs within the scales. They have wondrous voices, and their haunting songs travel over the waves as they sit on rocks, combing their hair while looking into mirrors.

Irish mer-people are called "merrows"—the women have webbed fingers, although they are kind and beautiful, while the males have green teeth and hair, red noses, and a jovial temperament. Merrows characteristically wear red caps, and if these are stolen, they cannot go back to the sea. Merrymaid is the Cornish equivalent, Meerfrauen or Meerjungfern the German, Meerminnen the Dutch, and Meerweiber the Scandinavian version.

There are many tales of bargains being struck between humans and mermaids, and of unions between them. One Scottish clan claims descent from a mermaid and a fisherman. Sometimes the mermaid will make promises in order to retrieve her comb or mirror, without which she is land-bound. These may take the form of granting three wishes, or even becoming wife to a human. But, there is always a price to be paid in return, and after a period of years—generally three, seven, or nine—the recipient of the mermaid's gifts must meet her again and be taken down forever into the watery depths. More usually, however, the enchanting mermaid will lure to a watery grave any unsuspecting human who comes upon her.

Sirens are a type of Greek sea nymph who, like mermaids, besides bewitching physical beauty, have the gift of magical song—so entrancing and irresistible that it could drive men mad and entice them to shipwreck on the rocks. Sirens lived on the island of Anthemoessa, and the hero Odysseus was the only man who heard them and lived, for he ordered himself to be tied to the mast of his boat, where he could not succumb to their deadly charms, while his sailors (their ears blocked with wax) guided the boat past the island. Consequently, a "siren song" has now come to be synonymous with dangerous seduction.

Mermaids may be connected with ancient and powerful creatrix goddesses, and the mirror and the comb are linked, in the Greek tongue, with the vulva. The ancients often regarded sexuality as sacred, and mermaids echo this.

The Kelpie

While all water sprites can be tricky, for the most part they are charming—but not so the Kelpie. This spirit appears as a gray horse, which may seem friendly at first, but this is only in order to entice the weary traveler onto its back. Once astride, the unfortunate is magically "stuck" and the Kelpie gallops into the water, submerging the rider until he or she drowns.

S ome Kelpies, such as the Shetland "Noggle," are more mischievous than malevolent, but can still be dangerous to humans. Even other fairies keep away from the Kelpie, and merely see it is an omen of death.

The Kelpie is essentially a spirit that haunts Scottish rivers. Often it can be heard wailing before storms arrive. Some stories tell of Kelpies wearing magical bridles that can be used by any human bold enough to steal them. By contrast, an ordinary bridle may be put on a Kelpie, although this is an extremely dangerous and difficult task. Once the bridle is in place, however, the Kelpie must do as it is bidden. One story tells how Graham of Morphie bridled a Kelpie and made him haul stones to build his castle. When the building was complete, Graham released the bruised and battered Kelpie, which galloped off into the river, pausing only to curse Graham and his clan. The Morphies never thrived in their new home, but found only misfortune.

Sometimes a Kelpie may appear as a handsome young man, and may attempt to lure young women away. The Kelpie can be recognized by the shells and watercress in his hair. He can also shape-shift into a rough, shaggy-haired human male, leaping up behind riverside riders and trying to crush them to death in his grip. More generally, the Kelpie may be the spirit of the river itself: unpredictable, hungry, and cruel.

The message of the Kelpie is certainly that Nature has a savage side and is to be respected. However, the horse also has other meanings, such as that of a "rider between the worlds," and so the Kelpie may be a shaman's steed, taking him on that perilous journey into the Otherworld, where he may learn great wisdom, or face death. Not all fairies are benign—and only the very wise or foolish antagonize the Kelpie.

The Nix

The Nix is a German water fairy who is very hard to spot, because he dives swiftly beneath the waters when approached. Like mer-people, he may wear a red cap.

In the 16th century, a Nix reportedly attended a fair at Laibach in Germany. Everyone was dancing in the town square near the fountain, when a handsome stranger joined the company. Those who shook him by the hand found it strangely damp and chill. Soon he asked the most flirtatious girl, Ursula, to dance with him. Everyone stopped to watch, so masterfully and yet so lightly did the young man guide his graceful companion. Faster and faster they whirled, until the company grew giddy watching them. No one noticed that they were getting closer to the edge of the dance area, until they were almost at the river. Suddenly, the stranger jumped into the waters, holding his companion, and she was never seen again. However, several fishermen reported seeing the Nix again, and thereafter the townspeople were wary of any stranger with a cold grip.

Nixen are not always fatal, although their eerie singing may induce madness, and they may steal human babes and leave a changeling behind. Sometimes they mate with humans and the resulting child is called an "urchin." Nixen can occasionally help humans, by warning of dangers in the water. They may also teach those brave enough to befriend them to play the fiddle in the manner of the fairies. However, to be taught "The Elf King's Tune" is to be doomed to fiddle eternally, unless a friend comes and cuts the violin strings from behind. The Nixie is the female counterpart, and she behaves in a similar seductive and threatening fashion to the Nix.

It is worthy of note that while female water sprites tend to tempt virtuous men, the male Nixen make off with flighty females! Might there be a double standard here? If so, it is not shared by the water fairies. The point is that Nixen and Nixies reflect our own human sexuality, which we may repress and which can mislead or betray us. Nixen and Nixies follow their own pleasure, and we too must follow our hearts if we are to find magic. But human and fairy is always a perilous alliance—make your own music, but shield your mortal ears from the song of the Nix.

The Melusine

Tales of the Melusine, or Melusina, occur in Scotland, France, Luxembourg, Germany, and many other countries. Here is a French version of her story.

Count Raymond and his friend Emmerick were hunting wild boar in the royal forest. Emmerick was following the trail ahead of Raymond, who came upon him struggling with the beast. Raymond killed the boar, but by mistake tragically slew his friend at the same time. Beside himself with grief, Raymond wandered the forest for days, unable to bear the thought of what he had done. Ragged and distraught, he at length came upon a wondrous fountain, beside which stood the loveliest woman he had ever seen. She comforted him, bathing his brow in the healing waters and offering him her wisdom. Raymond fell deeply in love with her and asked her to be his wife. She agreed, on one condition: that she could have Saturdays to herself,

and Raymond must never ask her what she did or where she went.

Raymond readily agreed to this request, and Melusine used her magical powers to build them a magnificent palace that encompassed her sacred spring. But in time Raymond grew curious. One Saturday he followed his wife to her chambers and spied on her as she bathed, when she turned into a water snake below the waist. Not wishing to lose her, Raymond kept quiet about what he had seen, until one of their sons burnt down a monastery. Raymond shouted at Melusine, 'See now what your evil has caused, you snake!' Too late he realized what he had done. Knowing now that he had broken his promise, Melusine resumed her snake form and disappeared.

This important story has, as its central message, the lost importance of the instinctual, fertile, wise, and creative Feminine. For hundreds of years the Goddess has been cast out, and women—with their connection to the realms of Nature, and their intuition—have been regarded as inferior. Today women are equal, and yet many have not reclaimed that wild, primitive, and fecund power.

All women have a Melusine within: a secret connection with the watery depths and the constant rhythm of the sea. Women's reproductive cycles correspond to the Moon, which also pulls the tides. Melusine can teach us how to recover our lost powers of healing, wisdom, sensuality and freedom. And for men who truly honor her and respect her wishes and desires, she promises joy and fulfillment.

The Naiad

Naiads are water nymphs, the spirits of streams, fountains, and wells in ancient Greece. In all probability, they were the old goddesses of Nature's sacred places, who later came to be regarded as something more trivial.

Each spring and each brook has its own laws, needs, and code of practice, in order to maintain its purity and usefulness. These were presided over by the naiad, whose permission was sought and whose rituals had to be observed before any incursion was made. Refusal to respect these natural laws has resulted in stagnation, poison, and a lack of fish and wildlife, as the fairies withdrew their vibrancy.

Naiads and other nymphs were sometimes mothers, or nursemaids, to the heroes of Greek myth. They are the guardians of the nurturing gifts of Mother Earth, flowing out in clear waters from between rocks, making the soil fertile. If you sit beside a stream or spring, you will soon become aware of the gentle presence of the naiad. She will be bless you if you clear any rubbish from her area.

The Nereid

Sometimes less friendly than naiads, nereides dwell in the sea, each of them ruling over a specific stretch of ocean. Originally there were fifty of them, all daughters of the sea-god Nereus. They wear headdresses made of shell and ride creatures called "hippocamps," which are part-horse, part-dolphin.

Like mermaids, nereides sing beautifully, although this is mostly to please the ear of their father, for they are credited with protecting sailors, rather than luring them to their death. However, they can be touchy and may inflict a human who sees them with anything from blindness to mutilation. Sometimes they bring madness or death by drowning, and they may covet human babies or even kill them. However, a kindly nereid may gift a child with magical protection.

Like the Selkie, nereides may inhabit seal-skins. In parts of Greece, descent is claimed from a nereid, and the hero Achilles was the son of a nereid called Thetis. However, these fairies will escape back to the sea as soon as they are able.

Lorelei

Lorelei is a lovely German water fairy, specific to the Rhine, where she lures men onto the rocks by playing her harp and singing. There are many such creatures, but one of them, at least, was once human.

Lorelei was a beautiful girl, so exquisite that no man could resist her. Other women became jealous and demanded that she be executed as a witch. She was brought before the bishop for trial, but he was so impressed with her sweetness and beauty that he could not bring himself to sentence her to death. Lorelei told him she had no desire for any man but her one true love, who had left her long ago. In fact, she wished to die, but the bishop decided instead to send her to a nunnery. He hired three knights to escort her, but while they were riding over a bridge on the Rhine, Lorelei suddenly slipped from among them, saying that she must take a last look at the waters. She looked down and cried that her long-lost love was in a boat below. The knights tried to stop her, but she slipped from their grasp. She flung herself into the waters and was never again seen in mortal form.

The Drac

Dracs are French water fairies who live beneath the Seine in an enchanted city. Sometimes they also live in caves, and may be glimpsed skating over the water on wooden plates.

D rac take the form of purple globes, but—like so many fairies—they can easily shape-shift and may become beautiful women to mate with men. Alternatively, they may rise from the waves in the shape of a golden chalice, but to reach for this means to risk being seized by the drac and dragged beneath the waves.

Like many fairies, dracs are believed to kidnap human mothers to act as wet-nurses for their children. These women are kept for seven years, and are unrecognizable when they are released. In the 13th century, a man known as Gervase of Tilbury met a woman who had such an experience, during which one of her eyes had been smeared with a grease that enabled her to see fairies. After her release she could still see them, and so was blinded in the offending eye by a drac.

Like all Otherworld encounters, meeting the dracs is an initiatory experience that can change a person for ever. The chalice is a feminine symbol, speaking of the womb and fruitfulness.

Finding Water Fairies

Do not be put off from attracting water fairies by the stories of
seduction, treachery, and danger that gather around these exquisite
creatures. Our culture is predominantly rationalistic and logical, and
therefore we tend to devalue and repress the emotional element.
Feelings that are denied may be dangerous indeed, for eventually
they can overwhelm us. Water is allied to feelings, and simply because
water fairies are close to this Element, they can help and heal us, if
we let them.

Water fairies also very much
express the enchantment and
allure of our romantic urges, and these
were demonized for many centuries.
Small wonder that water fairies have
become tricky at times, showing us that
we cannot escape our deeper natures.
However, our sexuality may be seen
as a gift of the Nature goddess, and as
such is deeply sacred. Water fairies
have some of the characteristics of the
great love goddess Aphrodite, who was
respected by gods and humans alike.

Your first step in drawing close
to water fairies is a pledge to be true
to your heart, and open to your own
emotions. Remember, being *aware* of
your feelings does not mean that you
have to act on all of them. Sometimes
the task is to face the pain of feelings
that cannot be fulfilled. This may hurt
at first, but only by being honest with
yourself can you eventually be free.
Water fairies can help with this,
enabling you to heal and move on as
your feelings transform.

On a practical level, be aware of water and its many blessings. Our planet and our bodies comprise 70 percent water. Be aware of the swirling tides, the unfathomed depths of the Pacific trenches, the silver ripples of rivers, and streams running inexorably seawards. Watch mists roll, clouds form, raindrops dance. Look after neighborhood waterways and lakes; help in water-clearing projects if possible; walk by water, linger, and reflect—in both senses of the word. Be aware also of your drinking water: its origins, its purity, and its gift to your body and mind.

Water holds images, is affected by thoughts and surroundings, and is tended and protected by its own special spirits—the many, varied and eternally beautiful water sprites. Respect this and learn from its magic.

Attracting Water Fairies at Home

Although you will doubtless want to go out and draw close to water fairies in their own habitat, it is good to start by affirming your closeness and respect in your own home. This is especially helpful if you want to invoke the spiritual essence of one of the fairies described on the previous pages.

METHOD

You will need to dedicate a small shelf or cupboard top as an altar to the water fairies.

1 Place on it some blue or green candles and a chalice—that is, a special glass with a stem, which honors the Element of Water. Fill the chalice with water from a special spring, lake, or stream, or from the ocean. An indoor fountain is an especially lovely idea and, if you have one, use spring water in it.

2 Add to your altar crystals such as amethyst, aquamarine, chalcedony, jade, moonstone, and sapphire. Seashells and stones that have been worn by water are also good choices. A stone with a hole in it is symbolic of the Mother Goddess and is especially suitable. You could also place there figures of aquatic creatures, such as fish, dolphins, and crabs, and any flowers that appeal, especially watery ones. Seaweed, willow artifacts, pictures, statues, and any material that resembles ripples, shells, or scales are all suitable, along with anything that reminds you of water.

3 You may like to burn joss-sticks scented with jasmine, lemon balm, eucalyptus, myrrh, rose, or vanilla, for these herbs were associated in old times with the deities of water.

4 If you wish to invoke a specific water-sprite attribute from the stories given earlier, be very clear about what it is that you wish for. For instance, you may want the wisdom and healing powers of Melusine, the seductiveness of a mermaid, the gracefulness of Undine, or the dancing gift of the Selkie. Place symbols of the appropriate fairy on your altar, such as a picture of a seal for the Selkie or a snake carving for Melusine. Be creative!

5 Light the candles and sit in front of the altar, clearly envisioning the gift coming your way and how life will be when you have it. Allow your imagination free rein. Also ask for protection, and promise to honor the water fairies—above all your own inner Feminine.

Attracting Water Fairies in the Wild

Drawing close to water fairies is first a matter of tuning into where they are likely to be. This is not hard: Any stretch of water that you find alluring is sure to be the habitat of fairies.

They can be found on a deserted beach, where the waves curl onto the shore, or swimming out on the tide. They haunt lonely stretches of rivers and lakes, and linger by springs. Trust your intuition—if you feel they are there, they will be close by.

METHOD

1 Before you go looking for water sprites, sip a special tea made from kelp and organic green tea. If you do not like the taste, just drink a little, to harmonize your body with the fairy beings that you are seeking.

2 Attune yourself to Nature and to the waters by really *being* there. Spend time alone with the elements, looking with the eyes of a child, playing in the shallows, skipping stones, and running your hands through the ripples. Try not to let your mind wander into thoughts about your work or family concerns—be totally, consciously present in the moment.

3 If you can play an instrument, bring it to the water's edge and play a tune, for water fairies are especially attracted to music. If you can sing, let your voice travel over the waves. It is important to strike the right note here—both literally and metaphorically. Be realistic about your talents; don't spoil things by disharmony. On the other hand, if you know you are really good at music, don't show off, because some fairies can be jealous.

4 Help aquatic animals, such as otters, and water birds, to please the fairies, or clean, clear, and tend a specific stretch of water and its plant life. If you are engrossed in watching the play of fish or frogs, you will be bringing just that kind of total attention to the here-and-now that is conducive to seeing fairies.

5 Look out around you for any signs that fairies are close by and consider them seriously. For instance, a curiously shaped stone or shell may be a fairy gift. Strange ripples in the water may be caused by a fairy presence. That movement you see from the corner of your eye is sure to be a fairy. Use your other senses too. What sounds are made by the rushing or lapping of the waters? Are they fairy voices? Linger on shores and banks, and sooner or later you will be blessed by fairy contact.

Meditation to Draw Close to Water Fairies

Open your heart to the water fairies and the boundaries between you and them will dissolve. Once you feel close to them, it will be easier to experience them in their own habitat.

METHOD

1 Relax completely, as described in the Introduction (see pages 34–35). Imagine that you are sitting beside a beautiful lake or a calm stretch of ocean. This may be a familiar place that you love, or it could be a place of your imagination. Take the time to settle in this spot. Fill in all the details of the environment. See the shimmering greens and blues of the waters, and all the other colors, reflected and refracted. Look at the azure sky arching overhead. Notice any plants and rocks, any features of the landscape—let your eyes dwell on these. See how close you are to the shore, where you are sitting or standing and what you are wearing. Notice in particular that you are wearing a large, beautiful emerald pendant, and that the stone is flat against your chest, over your heart.

2 Listen to the sounds around you. Can you hear the breeze, the birdsong, the sound of the waves? Smell the freshness of the air and the scent of water carried on it. Feel the pure, moist air on your face and the gentle wind fingering your hair. Enjoy all of this and make sure you feel comfortable and relaxed.

3 Now concentrate on the center of your chest, where your heart is. Breathe in the beauty of this place and allow your heart to be filled with love for it. Let your heart feel warm, open, and invigorated.

4 Remember the wonderful emerald hanging against your chest, close to your heart. As you feel a closeness and empathy with the beauty of the waters, so the emerald begins to shine. The warmth in your heart is flowing into the emerald, which pulses and glows in response. The radiance within the emerald is gentle, yet amazingly powerful. Soon you are aware that its wonderful light is stretching out over the waters, bathing everything in the purest green. The emerald green is reaching into the waters, mingling with them and shining outward again. The waters are becoming clearer, and you begin to see into their depths. What wondrous gifts and treasures do you find lying there? What magical beings are present?

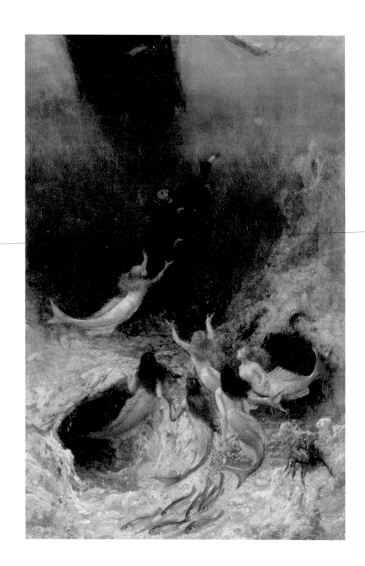

5 Invited by the emerald, called forth by the love in your heart, fairies are beginning to emerge from the waters. Watch as they come, strange and beautiful for the most part, others in shapes you may not have imagined. Continue to let the emerald light shine from you and to send a welcome from your heart.

6 Let the fairies emerge in their own way. They may remain far out on the waters, or they may approach closer to the edge. They may even come onto the land. Watch them as they appear, remaining serene and letting the emerald light of your heart continue to shine. Listen also, for the fairies may be talking, laughing, whispering, or— most likely of all—singing.

7 Invite the fairies close, asking if one of them will speak with you. If you are lucky, one of them will approach you. Listen to what the fairy says. If you like, you can ask questions—for instance, you may want to find out what you can do to enable you to draw closer to the water sprites in everyday life. The answers you get may be startlingly clear or they may not make

sense at first. Try not to puzzle over them for now.

8 When the time seems right, tell the fairies that you are bidding them farewell and that you honor them, and thank them for their presence. Say that you will visit them again. Let the emerald light slowly fade and shrink back into the crystal on your chest. Affirm that the emerald is closed, and that your heart is, for now, also closed. Touch the emerald and feel its coolness and solidity. Draw away from the scene.

9 Now come back to everyday awareness, patting your body all over to make sure that you are in the here-and-now. Make a note of all you experienced and any thoughts that have arisen in a special notebook.

10 You can repeat this journey as many times as you wish. More questions may occur to you, and you can ask your water-fairy spokesperson to answer them. Do not be surprised if the responses you get give rise to more and more questions, for that is the fairy way and is part of your quest. Happy journeying!

Mermaid Bath Spell for Beauty

Every mermaid knows, as she gazes into her mirror, that beauty is in the eye of the one beheld! If you believe that you are beautiful, there is no doubt that most people will be charmed by you.

METHOD

For this spell you will need a mirror—preferably a pretty one, with a handle. You will also need some spring water; some dried rose petals; some seaweed (which can be obtained in good health-food stores, or gather your own); a rose-pink candle; your favorite romantic CD (preferably instrumental rather than singing); and a natural sponge.

1 Make an infusion by filling a pan with spring water, bringing it to the boil, adding the rose petals and seaweed and then taking the pan off the heat. While the petals and seaweed are soaking, run a bath of warm water, light your candle in the bathroom, and start to play the CD, to build up an atmosphere.

2 Strain the infusion and add it to your bath. (Note: it is always a good idea to test for allergies 24 hours beforehand by placing a small amount of infusion on your inner wrist.) When the water is at the right temperature for you, get in, and close your eyes.

3 Bring to mind your own special water fairy that you met in the previous visualization (see pages 136–139) and ask her to be near. You may feel her presence as a slight tingling, and if you are lucky, you will see her.

4 Pick up the sponge and stroke your body all over, enjoying the sensuous experience. Tell your body it is beautiful (even if you are in the habit of thinking the opposite). Say, "From the sea came my life, from the sea came my body. Like the mermaids I am beautiful." Mentally ask your special mermaid to fill you with confidence and joy in your own sexuality.

5 Now pick up the mirror, look into your eyes and say, "I love you." Say this as many times as you can, while sitting comfortably in the bath. Maybe your mermaid will whisper something encouraging in your ear.

6 Complete the spell by thanking your mermaid and snuffing out the candle with a drop of water. As the water drains from the bath, let your consciousness return to normal. Wrap yourself in a big, soft towel and pamper yourself.

Meditation for Fairy Healing and Other Gifts

When you feel stressed and unhappy, an inner journey to the soothing watery depths can restore your perspective. Really things are not so bad! If you are sad or ill, there is much healing to be found with the undines; and if you have a problem, the Queen of the Waters has a boundless treasure-store of wisdom.

METHOD

1 Start your meditation in the same way as the previous one (see page 136). When the fairies appear, invite one to draw especially close to you, then ask her if you can accompany her to the underwater realms. Hold out your hand and she will take it.

2 You feel a change coming over your body. Look down and you will notice that scales have grown on you, and you have fins and a fish-tail. Responding to the undine's tug, allow yourself to sink beneath the surface of the water.

3 Amazingly, you find that you can breathe perfectly well as you swim. How wonderful it is in the underwater kingdom! The colors are indescribably beautiful, and all around you are fantastic creatures.

4 Now the surface is a distant memory and you are deep below the waves. Notice everything around you. As the daylight fades, its place is taken by a subtle, silvery glow.

5 You are coming to a wondrous palace, made of silver and encrusted with jewels. As you and your undine approach, the magnificent doors swing wide open to admit you.

6 You find yourself in a marvelous hall. This place could be on earth, except that it is much richer and more glorious than anything you have experienced. Tables encrusted with mother-of-pearl are laden with bowls of luscious fruits, and in the center of each stands a massive, jewelled chalice. You notice that much of what you see suggests love.

7 Ahead of you there are two thrones, made from shells and upholstered in emerald velvet. Upon them are seated the Queen of the Undines and her consort. Her long red hair streams down over her green gown beneath a crown of jade and coral. The King's crown is similar, but heavier, and his hair and beard are dark brown.

8 Letting go of the hand of your guide, you approach the thrones. The Queen speaks, in a voice both ringing and gentle: "Welcome to the world of the undines, my brave traveler! Draw close and tell me what you seek."

9 Go up to the Queen and bow your head with respect. Ask her for advice and, if appropriate, for healing of any wounds or illnesses (mental or physical) for you or others.

10 You will know when it is time to go. Give thanks and take respectful leave. Your guide will be waiting for you at the entrance to the hall, so take her hand again, to be led out of the palace. Rise slowly to the surface and resume your mortal form.

11 Thank your guide and say goodbye. Bring yourself thoroughly back to the everyday in the same way as before (see page 139), and record all that you have experienced.

Air
Fairies

The Element of Air

Air is the most insubstantial of the Elements. With each breath we take, Air gives us life. It is around and within us. It lends the sky its colors of blue, white, and gray, and it paints the sunset in flaming hues. Around the earth it spreads its gentle mantle, filtering the harshness of sunlight to lightness, brightness, and warmth.

Air itself is invisible. We can see its movement in the wind-stirred leaves, feel it brush our skin, and hear it whistling in our ears, but when the air is still, there is nothing to betray its subtle presence.

Air provides all that we see and hear, as light and sound waves travel through its medium. Our sense of smell is also a gift of Air, and with it we are connected to our past and a myriad of sensations, for smell is the most instinctual of senses. It connects to the reptilian brain-stem, so that one whiff of scent can evoke a spectrum of responses—a perfume, for instance, can whisk us back many years, vividly evoking emotions and images that we thought long past. So Air brings the gift of memory.

Air is associated with thought, communication, ideas, and movement. The generic name for the spirits of Air is "sylphs": mischievous and ethereal sprites who delight in their swiftness, freedom, cleverness, and unpredictability. They are the pure manifestation of the Element of Air— more mobile than quicksilver, and light as … air! These diaphanous beings want to make us wake up, set ourselves free and *think*—but not in the plodding way we have come to respect in our culture, where fact has to be set upon fact until we have built what we believe is an edifice of knowledge; the sylphs know that such "knowledge" isn't worth a feather when it comes to the etheric realms. Sylphs bring inspiration, revelation, new perspectives—and laughter. It may be easy to ignore them, to pull your hat down over your ears and stare at the ground, but the sylphs will tweak at your coat, whisper in your ear, and create a little monkey business around you, until you decide to look up and use your mind.

Aaah—breathe deeply and take flight with the sylphs.

Vila

Trees are the intermediary between earth and sky. There is a very special magic in them, and in a sense every tree forms a portal to the Otherworld. Small wonder that within the enchantment and shelter of the forest should be found one of the wildest, sweetest fairies of all—the Vila.

Images of the Vila live on today: Fleur Delacour, who captivates Ron Weasley in *Harry Potter and the Goblet of Fire*, is descended from a Vila. These Slavonic fairies have a special relationship with human beings. Each community traditionally had its own Vila, who guarded its harvest and taught the civilized arts of growing herbs and fruit and managing animals with kindness. Many social graces were also their gift, from music to honoring the dead. However, the Vily (plural of Vila) went into hiding when humans learnt to make war and became estranged from the land, thereby betraying not only the earth and her guardians, but also their own natures. The following is a tale of personal betrayal, involving a delicate Vila.

Long ago, in the morning of the world, when folk still existed in harmony with earth and sky, there lived a king and queen who had a son, a handsome but very lonely prince. He was the apple of his parents' eye, and when he came of age they arranged a magnificent banquet for him. From all over the kingdom people great and small came to honor the prince. Witches and fairies came too, and the young man was showered with gifts, but still he was sad deep within his heart, for true love had not yet come to him.

Night had fallen and the air was ringing with the sounds of the festivities when the weary prince slipped away to walk in the moonlit gardens of his palace. The grass glistened and the tree trunks stood silver in the darkness. Among them the prince glimpsed a shimmering movement. Intrigued, he drew closer and saw a tiny, exquisite fairy dancing in the shadows. As he approached she stopped and shrank behind a tree, but the prince called to her, "Beautiful sprite, come close to me, for I mean you no harm! Let me share in your joyfulness."

At this the fairy emerged, and the prince was sure she was bigger than when he had first seen her. "My prince," said she, "I was invited to your party, but my home is the forest and the wild lands. I am a Vila. True to my nature, I have remained here, among the trees. I dance to honor you."

The prince was entranced and moved towards the maiden, but as he drew close she disappeared. He searched for her until the moon went down, to no avail. That night he slept little, and all next day he longed for darkness to come. At the stroke of midnight he made his way down into the gardens and there, to his joy, once again saw the fairy dancing so gracefully. Again she seemed bigger; again they spoke for a while; and again she vanished.

The nightly encounters continued and the prince became paler and more listless by day, living only for his night-time trysts. As the moon waned, the fairy grew, until at the dark of the moon the Vila—now the size of a tall and slender maiden—lit up the grove with her radiance. No longer did she run from the prince. Instead each evening they walked among the trees and talked for hours, as the shadowy grove rang with the Vila's laughter. The prince fell deeply in love with the fairy, and when the first sickle of the new moon appeared in the sky, he sought her in the early evening. She

was bolder now, coming out while light yet lingered, and the prince fell on one knee, begging her to be his bride.

"Will you love me for ever?" asked the fairy.

"Yes, oh yes!" cried the prince.

"Then I shall be yours, as long as you remain true to your word," replied the Vila, and she took his hand and walked with him to the palace, where she was welcomed by the king and queen. Overjoyed, they arranged a magnificent wedding and bells rang throughout the kingdom.

For seven years the couple lived in blissful harmony. Then the old king fell ill and died, and the time came for the prince to assume the mantle of sovereignty. His first task was to bury his father with due honor, and to the funeral he invited magical creatures as well as humans. Among the guests was a vibrantly beautiful witch with long, wavy red hair, skin white as marble, and eyes of emerald green. The prince could not take his eyes off her. As he gazed at her, his wife tripped over her dress. "I am sorry," she said, "this dress is too long for me." The prince did not notice, for he was too busy sending sidelong glances to the stunning red-head. The Vila tripped again, and the top of her head, which had reached to just above his shoulder, now came only up to his chest. And within her sky-blue eyes was a look of unspeakable sadness.

Again she tripped, and again he ignored her and looked toward the red-headed witch. As he sat beside his wife in the carriage, sneaking glances out of the window, the Vila shrunk to the tiny proportions of the fairy he had first spotted in the garden grove. At last, with a final flicker like that of a snuffed candle, his beautiful wife disappeared, leaving behind an empty dress. But the prince hardly noticed. He called his attendants to tidy up and, with shaking heads, they complied as their master took the arm of the red-headed enchantress.

Within a week they were married, and within another week the prince realized his mistake. Soon he could see through the glamorous exterior to the hard, cold heart beneath, and it wasn't

long before he could stand the sight of his new wife no longer. Alas—too late he understood what he had done! He banished the witch from his court, and when night fell he went down into the palace gardens to look for his lost love. How pure the moon shone and how the trees glistened, all silvered against the shadows. And how wrenching the grief in the prince's heart as he called for the Vila, straining for a glimpse of her tiny, glittering form.

Every night for the rest of his life, the prince went down to the grove to await the return of his love. Years passed and he ceased to call her name—he merely waited all night, hoping she would come back. But she never did. With the rupture of his vow, the prince had severed the link with the fairy realm. One morning when he was a very old man, his attendants found him, lifeless, sitting against the largest tree in the grove. His palms lay open on his lap and on his face there was a smile, as if in death he had once more found his lost love.

WHAT THE STORY MEANS

Words are the gift of the Air Element. As vibration, they carry the creative essence of the Universe. A promise uttered travels through the subtle medium of Air and is binding. Air is the Element that best symbolizes clarity, purity, and trust. If a promise is broken, that trust may be gone for ever. Fairies abhor breaches of trust, and none more so than the Vila. This story also symbolizes the deep betrayal of the land and of our own inner natures when we turn away from the bond we have with Nature. The eventual price is isolation and emptiness. Reconnecting with the Vila can make us whole.

Odin, the All-Father

Odin is indeed a mighty spirit for, in days of old, he ruled in strength and wisdom over the gods of the Norsemen. These gods were the awesome Aesir, who dwelt in Asgard. Odin's domain is the vault of Heaven, which he rides on his eight-legged steed, Sleipnir, as he leads the Wild Hunt.

The Wild Hunt is a cavalcade of spirits—the souls of the dead that are borne away on the storm—and there are many versions of it, headed by different figures (see also Gwyn ap Nudd on pages 91, 252). Sometimes the Wild Hunt is believed to herd them into the Underworld. At other times, all the spirits pursue a quarry. This might be a magical boar or horse, or it might be the Moss Maidens, sprites that bear the essence of the autumn leaves,

torn from the trees. There are many accounts of the Wild Hunt in European folklore—for instance, at Fontainebleau in France, just before the Revolution—and those who witnessed it were usually doomed to die. Odin was reputed to prefer to ride forth in the days between Christmas and Twelfth Night, when peasants took care to leave out the last measure of grain as food for Sleipnir.

Although a god of battle, Odin is also known for his wisdom. He has two pet ravens: Hugin, which means

Thought, and Munin, which is Memory. Each day the ravens fly away into the skies and pick up information from far and near. At night they return, to perch on Odin's shoulders as he sits on his airy throne, and to whisper news of all they have seen. Odin is clad in robes of blue flecked with gray, to reflect the sky that is his home. At his feet sit his sacred hunting hounds, Geri and Freki, to which he feeds his own food, for this air spirit lives on ideas and has no need of solid nourishment to sustain him.

Odin obtained the gift of wisdom at the Fount of Mimir, in whose glistening depths all things are revealed. The guardian of the well demanded that he pay for this gift with one of his eyes, which Odin plucked from his head and flung into the waters of the well, where it still glows to this day. His remaining eye is symbolic of the sun. Since he received the gift of all-seeing, Odin has been melancholy, for he knows that all things must pass—even the time of his own kind.

One of the most well-known stories about Odin concerns the runes. This was a "discovery" rather than an invention, for the runes are magical symbols carrying a wisdom that is inherent within creation. They are also an alphabet, thus linking Odin with writing and communication. Odin hung for nine days and nights upon

Yggdrasil, a mighty ash tree that grew with its roots in the Underworld, its trunk in Middleworld and its branches in the realms of the gods. As Odin hung, suspended over an abyss, he entered a trance state in which he was granted even greater psychic powers.

This sky spirit has as his queen the breathtakingly beautiful Frigga, lady of the bounty of the earth and patroness of culture and marital love. Frigga is also an air fairy, tall and stately, crowned with heron plumes and robed in brilliant white. She is a cloud sprite and has the ability to see all, from her heavenly throne.

In another adventure Odin obtained the gift of poetry, by turning himself into a snake and penetrating an enchanted mountain, within whose vaults was kept

the precious Mead of Inspiration. He seduced the guardian of the mead, the beautiful Gunlod, so that she gave him a draught of the wondrous brew. Then Odin flew back, enriched, to the realm of the gods in Asgard.

Odin is thus a shape-shifter, and a spirit that bestows upon humans the attributes of eloquence, poetry and wisdom. He is a god of communication, self-expression, and clear thought—Odin brings the gift of being able to think the unthinkable and

change our minds, not from caprice but from widening perspectives. He is also a god of the dead, signifying that death is just another movement from one state to another, merely a progression in wisdom and experience. Seek him when the wild winds blow at midnight, and listen for the call of his ravens, deep within your soul.

The Valkyrs

The Valkyrs, or valkyries, were Odin's special battle-maidens. Their steeds were the clouds, their glittering spears were flashes of lightning. As the battle-cries died and the rooks circled down upon the carnage, the Valkyrs would ride in like the tempest, choosing the heroes among the slain to taste the joys of Valhalla (the hall of fallen champions) and stand shoulder-to-shoulder with the gods, when Ragnarok—the great battle that would end the world—had to be fought.

Beautiful creatures, the Valkyrs have flowing golden hair and arms white as the moon. They wear helmets of gold or silver, and red corselets. The love goddess Freya leads them whenever there is need for such a quest as theirs. The usual number given for the Valkyrs is nine, but who can count the magical dwellers in the fairy realm?

Beings of the Air never lose their love for the earth, and the Valkyrs regularly fly down, in swan plumage, to the shores of a secluded lake. There they fling off their snowy feathers and bathe. Many are the tales of mortal men who have surprised such beings in this way, taken their plumage, and had them in their power, to make them their wives. When the Valkyrs Olrun, Alvit, and Svanhit were taking their bath, they were spotted by three brothers, Egil, Slagfinn, and Volund (or Wayland). These men grabbed their feathers and forced the Valkyrs to marry them. For nine years the airy beings remained with their husbands, but inevitably they discovered where

their snow-shoes and headed
north in great distress to look
for the Valkyrs. But Wayland
waited—and his is another tale!

Couplings between men
and air fairies appear to be as
tricky as those between men
and water fairies—the problem
being that humans always try to
reduce everything to their level.
And no fairy can put up with
that for long. Air fairies can
never be tied down, but they
can elevate and inspire.

The Valkyrs bring the
message of the sweet release
of death. Perhaps they come
to convey that, however sore
the strife may be, beauty and
peace overlay it in the end.
Today we need the Valkyrs

their plumage—miraculously fresh and
shiny—had been hidden. Pulling it on,
they took to the air with cries of
freedom. Egil and Slagfinn donned

as much as, if not more than, the
warmongering Vikings. We
particularly need their courage
and breadth of vision.

Hermes

Hermes was recognized by the ancient Greeks as a powerful
messenger-spirit. The Romans knew him as Mercury, and he has
wings on his sandals that enable him to escape from the trouble he
often causes! Full of mischief, he once stole cattle belonging to his
brother, Apollo, but quick thinking saved him from retribution—
with his deft fingers, Hermes invented the lyre and gave this as a
peace-offering to his brother, who then laughed and forgave him.

One of the tasks of Hermes is to lead the souls of the dead into the Underworld, for he is the only one of the gods who is able to pass in and out of Hades without harm, since he can be many spirits in one—Hermes is the very essence of change, unpredictability, and adaptability.

Because thoughts are the power behind all types of fertility, Hermes was also honored as a god of procreation. Statues of him, called *hermeia*, were

erected in wayside shrines, showing his bust on top of a quadrangular pillar, with a phallus below. Respectful travelers would pour a libation of wine at the base of the statue. In even earlier times, the presence of Hermes was honored simply by a cairn of stones, to which travelers would add one stone, in homage, as they passed.

Hermes is the patron of thieves, and in this he exhibits the ambiguous nature of all true fairies. Human laws are very clear about property, but in the realm of the fairies there is an awareness that nothing that comes from the earth can truly be owned—all is lent, and all is to be shared. To those who wish to cling, and surround all they own with high fences, Hermes is a tricky sprite indeed, threatening to undermine all that is held dear. With a whisk of his traveling cape, Hermes reveals new perspectives, and then— whisk!—the scene changes again. For Hermes is truly wise, and brings the message that the only certain thing in life is change.

Leanan Sidhe

*The Leanan Sidhe (pronounced "Lanawn Shee") is an Irish spirit,
and one of the People of the Sidhe—the godlike creatures who
inhabited Ireland before the arrival of the Celts forced them into
another dimension. There may be one Leanan Sidhe, but probably
there are many.*

She is more easily known as Leanna, and is a bringer of creative inspiration, in true keeping with her identity as an air sprite. Like many fairies, her gift comes at a price. There are many tales of mortals who have been given the breath of genius by a Leanan Sidhe—here is one about a gifted composer.

The composer's name was Sebastian, and he was dashingly handsome, with a mane of black hair, dark eyes, and an air of aloof insouciance. He was sought-after in high society and could take his pick of the ladies, but their superficiality nauseated him, and increasingly he

took refuge in drink and debauchery. Whenever he came to a party he was fêted as a celebrity, although he became increasingly rude. This, however, did nothing to harm his popularity, and even though it was two years since his last successful opera, he was still welcome in the highest establishments.

At one magnificent social function he took refuge from his admirers in his host's study, taking with him a bottle of whisky. He was sinking into a drunken haze when he became aware of a woman in the room with him. He looked up and saw the most beautiful creature he had ever beheld. Her curtain of chestnut hair trailed

unfashionably, but enchantingly, down her back and she had an air of subtle knowingness, so that it was hard to determine her age. His caustic comment died on his lips as the woman smiled.

"I am Lady Leanna," she said. "I hope I am not disturbing you." She began to talk intelligently and wittily about his work, and Sebastian was entranced. While the ballroom extravaganza continued without them and the night grew late, they talked on and on. Lady Leanna was the wife of an elderly but very rich lord, and she soon proposed that she finance Sebastian in his career.

The next day, while Sebastian was nursing a hangover and wondering if he had imagined the events of the evening, there was a soft knock at his door. He opened it on his lovely companion of the previous night. His headache

vanished and the composer spent the rest of the day playing his heart out at his piano, while Lady Leanna sang in a high, haunting voice.

This was the first visit of many, and soon Sebastian was spending almost every day feverishly playing and composing, while Leanna stood beside him, singing, making suggestions, and encouraging him to work harder and harder. With her at his side, he wrote some of the most ethereal and wonderful tunes ever penned. Gone were his drinking habits, and the composer hardly even stopped to eat. When Leanna was with him, he put some of his most inspirational touches to his music, and while she was away he wrote reams and reams, so that he would have plenty to show her. His neighbors would hear his piano ringing out in the small hours, and often they heard him talking and laughing to himself. They never saw anyone visit him, and rumors began to circulate that he was mad, as were so many creative souls.

Three months after their first meeting, Sebastian's new opera was finished. He and Leanna sang it together, and as Sebastian sank back in his chair exhausted, Leanna said to him, "Sir, your work has stirred my heart. May I bestow upon you a kiss, as a reward?"

In truth, Sebastian had long dreamt that his chaste companion would give him more than her company, and he eagerly assented, raising his arms toward her. That was the last thing he ever did, for as their lips met, the fairy breathed in the composer's breath and with it sucked the soul from his body. His opera was published posthumously and performed to tumultuous acclaim. But no one ever found out who was the mysterious Lady Leanna to whom it was dedicated.

Leanna encourages mortals to become more than they are and to see the magic in daily life. Who can grow in this way and yet retain a hold on mortal life? Few, very few—and they are keeping their own counsel.

Arianrhod

Arianrhod is the powerful Welsh fairy queen who rules the circumpolar stars, known as Caer Arianrhod. Here is the crown of the North Wind, a ring of jewels in the sky, home in life-between-life to souls who fly there to be healed and to prepare for their next life on earth. Poets, while they sleep, go to Caer Arianrhod in their dreams, and the Goddess bestows inspiration upon them. And what is the price to be paid? True adoration of the Feminine.

In the brilliant morning of the world, women held great honor and power. Only by right of the Goddess could a sovereign rule the land, and young men were given their arms by warrior witches—so Celtic legend states. But as patriarchy took over, the Feminine was debased, and this is one of the reasons why so few of us can now see fairies.

Mighty queen that she was, and is, Arianrhod refused to be brow-beaten. She would not name her son (Lleu), as was the mother's prerogative, if it meant losing her matriarchal rights, nor would she give him weapons. When she was tricked into doing so by her brother, Gwydion, she swore that her son would have no bride.

Arianrhod sounds harsh indeed, but there was wisdom to her deeds, for she foresaw that the future of a world bereft of respect for the Feminine, the earth, and the intuitive element was bleak indeed. Alas, her wishes were flouted when Gwydion used his own magic to produce a bride for Lleu, made from blossom of the oak,

meadowsweet, and broom. So it seemed that men had conquered even Nature, making of her images to their own base desire.

Thus Lleu, against his mother's advice, married his beautiful "Flower Face," whose name in Welsh is Blodeuwydd. But this also ended in tragedy, for Blodeuwydd—though made by men—was a goddess in her own right and her heart could not be constrained. She fell in love with another man, Gronw, and together they planned to murder Lleu.

Lleu was slain, yet he magically revived, and Gronw was also slain. Blodeuwydd became an owl, symbol for wisdom. The owl is a bird long associated with goddess power, for it was also sacred to Athene, Greek goddess of wisdom. It flies by night and, in the darkness, what is invisible to normal sight is revealed to the owl. And so the tale comes full circle, with the wisdom of the Goddess, the inner knowing of the natural world and the long sight of the Fair Folk. After all the trials and tribulations, in the cycles of Nature lies the only path to making sense of a senseless world.

On a clear night, if you live in the Northern Hemisphere, cast your eyes towards the northern constellation, shining bright as crystals. These stars never sink below the horizon, even in midsummer. Can you glimpse the towers of Caer Arianrhod, topped by glimmering stars? If you live in the Southern Hemisphere, never believe Caer Arianrhod is beyond your sight. Wherever stars bejewel the velvet of midnight, there Arianrhod's realm can be spotted by those in tune with their inner nature. Look up and forget what science has told you of the stars. How can we know that is not yet another illusion? Can you recognize the true home of your soul? Then you are surely fairy-gifted.

Lilith

Here we have another female air spirit—with attitude! Lilith is spoken of in Hebrew legend as Adam's first wife, but she is a version of the Sumerian Lilitu: a wild spirit of wind and storm, who flew through the darkness to bring nightmares.

Lilith is a spirit who has been thought ill of because for centuries she embodied something that was culturally unacceptable—an independent woman! Lilith is the voice that whispers rebellion in the ear of every submissive wife; the voice that encourages retaliation in the abused and suppressed; the voice that calls the ignorant to get educated and act.

She is no easy sprite, because she has a knack for turning over the neatly raked, prissily planted flower bed, to reveal all the worms wriggling underneath. The knowledge she brings may be unwelcome at first, but usually we are the stronger for it. Do not fear Lilith, if you hear her murmurs as you settle to sleep. Listen to her, and show her respect. Then she becomes constructive and will bring you the gift of a unique creativity.

Thoth the Wise

So many air spirits are linked to wisdom, and none more so than Thoth, the ibis-headed Egyptian god. Thoth is, in fact, a mighty creator spirit from long before dynastic times. By the sound of his voice he created gods and goddesses, and in turn, with their singing, they kept the Sun moving in the sky. Occasionally Thoth is seen with a baboon's head, perhaps because baboons chatter to greet the sunrise. The power of the spoken word is featured repeatedly in creation tales and magical practices.

Thoth was also lord of the Moon, although in this context the Moon is more of a measuring device, for Thoth invented the calendar. He was opposed to injustice, and used his brilliance to unite the lovers Nut and Geb: Nut was goddess of the sky and had married her brother Geb, the earth, in defiance of their grandfather, the sun god Ra. Ra commanded their father, the air god Shu, to separate them, and decreed that Nut should bear no children in any month of the year. So Thoth played draughts with the Moon and won a seventy-second part of the Moon's light, which he turned into five intercalary days (days inserted in the calendar). Thus there were five days in the year during which Nut could give birth, and she brought

forth Osiris, Horus the Elder, Isis, Set and Nephthys.

Later, when Set conspired to overthrow his brother Osiris and murdered him, Thoth remained loyal to Isis, Osiris' wife, and often worked magic with her. Osiris became King of the Underworld and, in common with Hermes (see page 160), it was Thoth's

task to be part of the admission of souls into his kingdom. These souls were weighed in scales against the feather of truth, to see whether they were light enough to enter the sacred kingdom.

In a quest for truth and justice, Thoth is a wonderful ally. His truth may not be a literal truth, but rather the power of self-knowledge, the realization the soul has of its destiny and purpose. Thoth's justice knows no retribution, but balances the scales between the needs of each. Call upon him when you need to feel benevolently detached from a situation; when you need to think clearly or be honest with yourself; or when you need to be "clever," such as when taking an exam—remember, he out-foxed the sun god Ra himself!

White Buffalo Woman

Native Americans tell of how the secrets of the peace pipe were revealed by White Buffalo Woman, who appeared on a mountain to two braves. She was clad in white and bedecked with glorious jewels. Out of a cloud she emerged, and the hunters stood in awe before her. When she looked his way, however, the less disciplined of the two men rushed toward her, to embrace her. Smiling, she received him into her arms, and the white cloud again arose to enfold them. When it cleared, the woman stood alone, with the skeleton of the hunter at her feet.

Humbled, the remaining brave ushered her to his village, and as they walked she assured him that his companion had received exactly what he sought. On arrival at the village she initiated the tribe into the mysteries of the peace pipe, which is the union of male and female, through the breath of spirit. The round bowl represents the Feminine, the stem is the Masculine, and the smoke that moves between is the ethereal connection. After sharing the pipe with the tribe, she bade them always to honor Mother Earth, then transformed herself into a white buffalo and disappeared.

The buffalo was much honored among Native Americans, for it supplied all their needs: flesh for nourishment, skin for clothing and tents, and bones for utensils. In effect it embodied the powers of life. Thus the fairy's transformation into a buffalo was a sign of great power. The encounter of the impetuous brave with the fairy realm has much in common with many other tales, for while he was enveloped in the white cloud of the air spirit, human time had no meaning, and what was but a minute to his waiting companion was to him hundreds of years, as he grew old, died and the flesh fell from his bones.

One of the most important points of this story, however, is the sacredness of sexuality, and the need for good communication and rapport in order for it to work. The smoke in the peace pipe means many things. It may be the smoke given off by the fires of passion or the intoxicating scent of love itself. Most importantly it is the breath of words, spoken from the heart, seeking true understanding and union.

The Seven Ravens

This Grimms' fairy tale is about the powers of Air. There was once a couple who had seven sons, but they yearned for a daughter. Eventually a girl was born, but she was sickly, so the boys were sent urgently to the well for water. While there, they argued and dropped the jug. They took so long that their father complained about them and said he wished they were all ravens, whereupon they turned into birds and flew over his head, away into the distance.

Distraught though the couple were to lose their sons, their beautiful daughter gave them joy as she grew. At length, however, she wanted to search for her brothers. She turned to the power of the elements and asked the Sun for help, but he burnt her; she asked the Moon, but he deceived her. She asked the friendly stars, and one gave her a chicken bone, to release her brothers from the glass mountain where they were captive. Sadly the girl lost the bone, so she bravely cut off her own finger to use as a key.

This story is more complex in its full-length version, with many different symbolic meanings. One thing is clear: we should be careful what we wish for, in case the sylphs hear us! The father's wish was made in anger and was misguided, and for this he suffered the loss of his sons. However, the wish of the raven-son was wise, so he and his brothers became human again. The bravery and resourcefulness of the sister appealed to the fairies, and the ring signified memory—the unseen, enduring thread that the sylphs help to spin.

Once inside, she spotted seven dishes of food and seven cups. She ate and drank a little from each one, and in the last she dropped her mother's ring. Then the air was filled with a whirring sound. She hid behind a door as the ravens returned. "Who has eaten from our plates?" they demanded. "We know it is a mortal." Then one of them spied the ring and cried, "God grant our sister may be here, and we are released!" The girl then stepped out, the boys became human again, and all went home to a reunion and great rejoicing.

The Four Winds

The four winds are very special powers, each having their own monarch and band of sprites. The four winds come from each of the four quarters, and are associated with a specific Element.

This may seem hard to understand, because surely all winds are basically the *Air* Element? However, the winds are, to some extent, *messengers*—they bring signs from another world. Like the association of Air with communication and travel, the winds can also be seen to open a portal to a specific quarter of the Otherworld.

In Western occultism the names of the winds are used as part of magical invocations. When the magic circle is cast, made of mind-stuff and intended to protect the practitioner and contain the power, the four Elements are summoned at the four quarters and are asked to act as guardians. These four quarters are called The Watchtowers, and each of them is attended by a mighty wind. Often, as this wind is called upon, it can be felt to blow into the circle with all its attendant spirits, and with the "feel" of the Element in the question being invoked.

Magical practitioners have been aware of these powers probably since the dawn of time. The four winds are still known today by their ancient Greek names: Eurius (pronounced

"Yoo-rus") is the East wind, bringing with it the powers of the Element of Air; Notus is the South wind, or the Element of Fire; Zephyrus is the West wind, or the Element of Water; and Boreas is the North wind, or the Element of Earth.

All of these links are, of course, built up by associations with the natural world, from a spirit of "where you are." That is what contact with the fairies is all about: a true closeness to Nature, so that eventually she twitches aside her veil and other realities become visible. The links that we adopt are based on a position in the Northern Hemisphere, although other viewpoints are possible—for instance, the Lakota Natives equate South with Water. With that in mind, if you live in the Southern Hemisphere feel free to adapt: Fire/Notus for you will be in the north, as that is the warmest quarter, and Earth/Boreas in the south. As always, follow your intuition and go with what feels right.

Eurius, Lord of East and Air

Eurius and his youthful lady—
for the lady is, of course, equal
in importance to the lord—
open the portals on the dawn, and
their own Element of Air. The sylphs
(see page 146) come flying through with all their
gifts. However, in this case they are on a mission!
Their purpose is to guard the circle against all lack
of clarity and excessive and inappropriate emotion.

They are a great help when you need to concentrate on a ritual, although they can also make you giggle. Luckily the Goddess loves reverence with mirth. They can also help you when you need something ordinary, like a clear road ahead; when you are in a hurry; or when you need success in an exam or interview. Simply imagine the doors to their realm spreading wide, and ask them for their help.

Eurius comes with dizzying, mountaintop vistas, with the sound of the winds rushing through the trees, and with the sometimes gentle, sometimes brilliant light of dawn. Eurius is freedom from prejudice, routine, and all the concepts that hold us back. His is the realm of new beginnings— turn to him when you need a little confidence and a lot of hope.

Notus, Lord of South and Fire

*The hot breath of warmer climates comes in with Notus and his
dazzling queen, as they open the way to the essence of midday. With
them come the salamanders (see page 200)—irrepressible beings of
flame and energy, all of which they are determined to put to work.*

Salamanders bring inspiration and enthusiasm. While sylphs can help you think clearly, salamanders come with those flashes of pure brilliance that hail from we-know-not-where. These beings come with intuition, and with passion. They set the heart and mind aflame, and enable us to feel we can do anything! In ordinary life, when you need an injection of enthusiasm, ask for Notus to open his doors and let the salamanders fill you with courage and optimism.

Notus comes with the hot breath of the sun-baked desert, and with all that is exotic and colorful. He also brings vistas of hilltop beacons, fireworks, welcoming hearths, and even home cooking. It all depends when you are calling him, and why. Notus is freedom from the negative and all the "I can'ts" that we keep repeating. His is the realm of belief—turn to him when you need some oomph, and when you want to feel playful.

Zephyrus, Lord of West and Water

Zephyrus and his gentle lady bring with them the repose and tranquility of evening. With them come the undines (see page 104), diving and splashing. Now they arrive with all the poetry and sweetness of their natures. They bring true feeling that comes from self-knowledge.

Undines' understanding and compassion foster bonds between human beings and ensure that we remain connected to the real meaning of our "tribe" and traditions. They bring love and empathy. As the undines arrive we feel a sense of understanding and relaxation, an "all right-ness." In normal life, when you need closeness, affection and to feel really heard, ask for Zephyrus to let his doors swing wide to enable the undines to help you.

Zephyrus comes with the softness of the rain and the mystery of the westering sun. The Isles of the Blest, where some say the dead go to rest, are in the west, hence its connection with the past. However, Zephyrus can also be strong and rousing, driving the showers and heralding transformation. Zephyrus is freedom from loneliness and any feelings of not belonging. His is the realm of true emotions—turn to him when you need the release of tears or laughter and want to feel cared for.

Boreas, Lord of North and Earth

Boreas and his noble queen bring with them the solidity and protection of earth. With them come the gnomes (see page 235), marching purposefully. Now they come with a down-to-earth practicality. These are no-nonsense beings who believe in being organized.

The gnomes keep our feet on the ground and make sure that our self-preservation is intact and that we only attempt the possible. As the gnomes arrive we feel a comforting sense of being grounded and protected. In normal life, when you need an injection of common sense and some luck with money or property, ask Boreas to open his doors to enable the gnomes to come on a rescue mission.

Boreas comes with the harsh blast of the snowy wastes, but also with the ancient wisdom of the cave and the solitary standing stone. Call on him for certainty and security.

The Griffin

The griffin is a fantastical creature of the fairy realm, which comes mainly from the Middle East. It is any fairy that is part-mammal and part-bird, though it is usually part-lion and part-eagle. The Hippogriff in the Harry Potter *stories is a griffin, and this creature is very touchy and rather aggressive!*

Like most fairies, the griffin does not tolerate bad manners; but unlike many, it is built to retaliate. Fairies and their endeavors need protection, and the griffin's function is to repel intruders and avenge hurt. It is a gentle guardian, but is quite ruthless in pursuit of revenge. Often a griffin's

actions will appear as natural phenomena, such as storms.

Because the griffin is half-animal, half-bird, it symbolizes the union of matter and spirit. It is ever-watchful, ever-just, rarely forgiving. The Assyrians believed that the angel of death was a griffin. This fairy creature is famed for its acute hearing, and its gift to those it approaches is the ability to hear what others are *truly* saying, as opposed to the mere words, which often mislead. If you feel a griffin has drawn close to you, this is a time of great power. Look for lightning in the sky and a special mighty feather, to indicate its passage.

The Sphinx

Another composite fairy, the sphinx embodies mystery. To the Greeks it had a woman's head and the body of a winged lion, while the Egyptian sphinx had a male head, or that of a ram or hawk, linking it to the griffin.

The composite nature of the sphinx indicates the deep knowledge that comes from a union of spirit, instinct and intellect. In myth, this being is often encountered as a guardian to ancient mysteries. To test the worthiness of any who approached, the sphinx would demand the passing of some test, or the solution of a riddle. To fail at this usually resulted in death, frequently by being devoured by the vengeful sphinx.

The symbolism behind this relates to understanding, and the use of knowledge. Partial knowledge, when arrogantly applied, can lead to being "devoured" by the consequences of ignorance. This applies today where scientific knowledge is used without regard to spiritual meaning.

If you are faced with many conundrums in life, suspect the involvement of the sphinx. Do not panic! It may be a call to further education or mental expansion. The sphinx is the carrier of prophecy, and is there to challenge and inspire.

Finding Air Fairies

Air is all around us, giving us life second by second, even though we are largely unaware of it. Further than this, Air carries the power of the Word—in other parlance, of the vibration of power that initiates creation. Sound travels through air, communication is airborne. The delight of music comes the same way. "Inspiration" derives from the Latin spiritu, *meaning "to breathe."*

Air is thought, education, understanding, and freedom. All that we think issues forth into the air, changing the atmosphere around us, and while for the most part the effects are trivial and temporary, very black and potent thoughts over a period of time can seriously contaminate the air.

Sylphs may be tiny or huge and mighty, coming on a gentle breath or a tempest. They work to cleanse and protect the atmosphere, creating and moving clouds, keeping all in motion, all in balance. They are also involved wherever there is mental effort, bringing us understanding and healing. Sylphs are connected with no specific physical life, and so are among the freest of all the fairies. They can be found anywhere, and some of the most developed of their kind may be equated with angels, for they are messengers of the spirit. As guardians and healers. sylphs work to ease suffering, and are attracted to children because their hearts are light, yet vulnerable.

Needless to say, awareness of the beauty and delicacy of the air is a first step towards summoning these beings. Ensure the air in your home is fresh

and mobile. Choose joss-sticks with great care, for offering the sylphs anything bad-smelling will have the opposite effect! Support projects that seek to cleanse the atmosphere. Like undines, sylphs are drawn to music, but their favorites are pipes and flutes. Whistling can also call them up.

Above all, let your own thoughts be pure. This does *not* mean that you should repress any negative feelings, but try to see them as a burden you do not need and let the sylphs waft them away. When you feel these fairies close by, your troubles will dissipate anyway and you will smile. Use your mind, too. Communicate with others, be prepared to learn new things, be open and truthful. Respect the power of telepathy and be prepared to develop it. In time your own special sylph will attend you, to help you grow.

Air Fairies at Home

Experiencing these creatures in their own habitat is gloriously uplifting, but you can start at home by affirming your affinity with them. This will be especially beneficial if you wish to attract one of the beings already described.

METHOD

You will need to set aside a small shelf or something similar as an altar (see page 36).

1 Cover your altar with a white or pale blue cloth, if you wish, and also choose candles of pale blue or white. Incense is desirable on any altar, but for air fairies especially so. Invest in a censer, which you can swing, thereby enabling you to permeate the air with fragrance. Essences that are especially appropriate are orange bergamot, lavender, lemongrass, and pine, although naturally you can go with whatever feels right. An oil burner is also wonderful, allowing the gentle fragrance to rise.

2 On your altar place anything that reminds you of the Element of Air, or anything special that you may have found in a place that you felt to be full of these creatures. Feathers are an obvious choice, along with wind-borne seeds such as sycamore keys, "will-o'-the-wisps," and even dandelion "clocks." Pictures of cloudy or aerial scenes are good, as are figures of birds. As for crystals, choose jasper, aventurine, or agate—blue-lace agate is especially appropriate. Certain flowers also have traditional "airy" associations, including clover, dandelion, eyebright, lily of the valley, and meadowsweet. Whether the fairies of those flowers would agree probably depends on several things—again, go with what you feel.

3 To attract the blessing of any of the spirits mentioned on the previous pages, honor him or her on your altar. For instance, if you wish for wisdom, ravens and runes invoke Odin. Stars bring with them the eternal mysteries of Arianrhod. If you wish for the inspiration of Leanan Sidhe, then a mini-version of a musical instrument will help your magic.

4 Because the air sprites have such affinity with thought and communication, they can help you with all matters connected with them. Place on your altar a pen—especially a quill pen—and a scroll, to speed up correspondence. You could even put your computer disks there, underneath a crystal.

Air Fairies in the Wild

The sylphs are perhaps the easiest to find of all fairies, because they are everywhere. Places where there has been great evil, such as the sites of concentration camps, will be shunned by many of them, and those that are there will be concerned with the purposes of cleansing and healing, rather than human communication; other areas that are being heavily polluted by humans, such as certain smoky industrial sites, are unlikely to be favored by them. Apart from that, wherever you breathe, the sylphs are there.

METHOD

1 For easiest contact with these wonderful beings, climb to the top of a hill, preferably on a clear day, when the air is fresh and flowing. Open your heart to the purity of the breeze and be aware of every touch, every caress, every murmur. Sometimes the air will go still, and you will feel a swirl of the breeze around your shoulders and in your hair, to tell you a sylph is near. Watch the clouds closely, looking for pictures and shapes—what do they tell you? Is there a message? See if you can make the clouds form the shape that *you* want; you can even do this from your window. If this happens, it is very likely that you are making telepathic contact with the sylphs.

2 Flying a kite is another way to be close to the sylphs. Watch as the wind plays with the kite, feeling the tug and counter-tug, the swooping and diving. As your kite flies, you will probably spend more time looking at the sky than you have for many days put together. Become attuned to the ways of the winds and the fairies that empower them.

3 Playing pan-pipes or a flute is another sylph-friendly thing to do. Or whistle an old tune as you sit under a tree. Choose a still day for this, and enjoy running through the tune a few times. Soon you will feel a slight breeze and the leaves will rustle or the dust swirl, as the sylphs arrive.

4 The air fairies may take the shape of a bird or butterfly. To show they have been they often leave the gift of a feather, or you may smell a fragrance. Either way, you are fortunate, for your dialogue with the sylphs has begun.

Air-Spirit Spell for Exam Success

Use this spell to empower a crystal in order to bring you success in a forthcoming test or examination.

METHOD

You will need a small piece of blue-lace agate for this spell, and a feather. Almost any feather will do, but one you have found yourself is best. Try to ensure that any feather you use has been humanely come by.

1 Take your feather and crystal with you to a peaceful place in Nature, for instance, under a tree. Make sure that you are private. Alternatively, you may do this spell at your window.

2 Use your feather to attune you to the world of the sylphs. Imagine it when it was helping the bird it belonged to soar high in the sky. Close your eyes and visualize this lightness, this freedom. Call on the sylphs.

3 When a special breeze announces the presence of the sylphs, hold out your piece of agate and imagine all the clarity and swiftness of their world entering it. Ask the sylphs to empower your crystal with their wisdom, insight, and buoyancy.

4 When you feel this has finished, give thanks and keep your crystal with you while you study and take your exam. You can re-empower it at any time you wish.

Air-Spirit Spell for Communication

This spell will attract communications to you from the outside world; whether by phone, text message, letter, or e-mail.

METHOD

You will need a little essential oil of lavender (this should be a pure oil from a reputable source). Invest in a special bottle or jar, then place plenty of oil in it, so that you have enough for your spell. Lavender is a very gentle, safe oil, but you can dilute two drops to a teaspoon of sweet almond oil, if you wish.

1 Proceed in a similar way to that described for "charging up" your agate (see page 190). Lavender has an affinity with the sylphs and so they will come to you. Whistle a tune if you wish.

2 When you feel that special breeze or see a bird or butterfly come close, ask the sylphs to speed communication in your life and make it flow smoothly, like the wind. Imagine the phone ringing, texts arriving, letters falling on the mat, and your e-mail box full of messages. Thank the sylphs for their help and hard work.

3 Anoint yourself with a little oil on your temples, wrists, and ankles. Place some on a small scarf and tie it to your computer cable, then put a little oil on your phones and mailbox (careful, it's very greasy!).

4 Wait to be bombarded with communications.

Meditation to Enter the World of the Air Sprites

Once you become aware of the air sprites, you will hear their silvery voices all around you. This meditation is designed to allow your spirit to feel free to make contact. As you do it, be aware that many people have their own special sylph, who is there to inspire them. Be aware too that this being is a guardian, akin to the concept of a guardian angel, and is there to awaken your mind and protect you.

METHOD

1 Relax completely, as described in the Introduction (see pages 34–35). If you can find somewhere safe and secluded outside, so much the better. Now see yourself walking through a majestic, classical city, along a sweeping boulevard. Here there are no cars to disturb the atmosphere. You are robed in white and on your feet are cool sandals. On each side of you rise magnificent white buildings, with Doric columns, platforms, and large arched doorways. In and around these buildings other beings glide, clad also in white. Their movements are so smooth that it seems almost as if their feet do not touch the ground.

2 You are aware of the breeze on your cheek—it has a special gentleness, a way of playing with your hair, that feels intimate. The air is the clearest, cleanest air you have ever encountered, and yet it is pleasantly warm. There is an elusive floral fragrance all about you. Although you are moving uphill, your feet are so light it almost feels like you are flying.

3 The road curves round to the right, narrowing and going more steeply uphill. You follow it. It spirals its way higher and higher. You pass many wonderful buildings, but gradually these thin out until your path is lined with trees. These toss and turn in the wind, but the air around you is, for the most part, still.

4 The trees are now beginning to spread out, and you become aware that you have climbed very high. Soon you find yourself on a wide, grassy plateau. You walk to the edge and look out over a vast panorama of hill and dale, white colonnaded city, blue sky, and fluffy clouds. The breeze is intermittent, playful and sometimes seems to be laughing and dancing.

5 You hold out your arms, and the wind begins to blow. You feel it all around you, this way and that, tugging at your clothes. Now you begin to catch glimpses of swirling figures, so slender, so light, swooping and weaving in the blustering air. You can feel them brushing your skin, and their laughing words are becoming audible.

6 Now you notice that the white clouds are banking up and drawing together. Awed, you watch as a mass of cloud comes towards you, changing shape many times as it approaches, until it hangs in the air before you in a pearly mist.

7 You watch, as this mist takes the shape of a magical, airy, white-robed being. This being has come especially for you. With it comes an atmosphere of great peace, but also excitement, as if all things are possible. This may be your guardian spirit or it may be some other sprite. Around this being the other sylphs dance and play, and everything about him or her—robes, hair, even limbs—is continually in wind-borne motion.

8 You may hear the voice of this spirit, musical as the breeze, or you may have to be the one to ask questions. Do not hesitate, for these are communicative spirits who thrive on interchange. However, do not expect all the answers to be easy to comprehend. Take the time to ask as much as you want, and try to listen to the answers even if they seem ambiguous. Don't be afraid to laugh— not all that you hear will be deep or serious, for this is a light-hearted and playful being who has seen all that is wrought by humans and often finds it very amusing.

9 When the time feels right, take your leave with thanks and make your way back down the spiralling path. The sylphs come with you now, swooping and diving around you, guiding your footsteps as you make you way along the rocky path, between the trees, down, down, with buildings now on either side, until you find yourself turning left onto the wide avenue along which you made your way into the city.

10 As you walk, the buildings become more indistinct, the aspect blurs and darkens— until you find that you are back in everyday awareness. Record everything important in your special notebook—you may find this goes especially smoothly with the help of the sylph you have brought back with you.

Meditation to Receive the Gifts of the Sylphs

Once again, this exercise requesting the sylphs to empower you with their gifts is best performed outside, if possible.

METHOD

1 Close your eyes, relax, and see yourself walking along the same wide boulevard as before (see page 192). Notice the magnificent sculptures, the cleanliness and freshness, the culture and tranquillity. There seem to be more people around, white-robed and moving smoothly. You are also aware of the sylphs around you, perpetually in motion.

2 Toward you another robed figure is approaching, glowing with its own inner light. You recognize the being you met on the grassy plateau, who now beckons you close. The sylphs gravitate to the spirit, dancing around it.

3 The being asks what you have come for—what knowledge, what skill. Say clearly what you seek: it should be a mental skill, such as writing poetry, the gift of prophecy, the ability to see a situation clearly, or to look into the mind of another.

4 Your guide will tell you that your request will be granted, but first there is work to be done. You are led into one of the magnificent buildings. You follow your guide along white marble halls and into a marvelous room with a vast, domed ceiling.

5 Your guide leads you to what appears to be a massive table, but you find yourself looking down at a map. It is as if you are staring down at the earth from the height of an eagle in flight. Some places on the map are bright and others are dim. Your guide explains that the dim areas are places where you have thought negatively, the bright ones where you have been creative. As you watch, you realize that you are being shown the truth about times and places in your life. Take as long as you wish over this. Work at turning the dim places into bright ones, through positive thought; imagine the light growing.

6 When your efforts are completed, your guide takes you over to a large cabinet with intricate engravings, draws out a crystal, a scroll, a casket, and a key, and asks you to choose the one that will best help you toward your goal. The other treasures are returned to the dim interior.

7 Your guide takes you out onto a balcony, where a far-flung sunlit panorama spreads before you. He or she takes your treasure and breathes upon it. As this happens, the wind rises mightily, flapping your robes about your legs, and you feel a tremendous surge of power.

8 Your gift is restored to you and you are led back out of the building. Take your leave of your guide, with thanks, as the sylphs dance in the air. Walk down the road, until the scene grows dim and you find yourself back in everyday awareness.

9 Note all that you have thought or seen in your notebook, especially the nature of your gift, for it is symbolic and important.

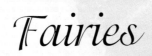

Fire
Fairies

The Element of Fire

Fire is dynamism, Fire is heat, Fire is change. It brings both creation and destruction. Without Fire all would be inert and frozen. In all its forms, Fire is what makes life exciting, and it is often the energy that moves us on to new phases, when suddenly everything looks different.

In some ways Fire is the most difficult Element to work with, because it is so powerful, and these energies can easily get out of control. However, it is important that we *do* become aware of the fire fairies. We need them in order to get in touch with the passion and creativity within ourselves. We also need to bring Fire more consciously into our lives, for it is largely missing in a modern environment. Open hearths have disappeared from homes, and cooking is rarely done over an open flame. The Fire elementals, when carefully approached, can warm our hearts and invigorate our lives.

Fire spirits are called salamanders, and they are present wherever there is Fire, both seen and unseen. Despite their name, they do not by any means always appear as reptiles. While the dragon is one of their forms, they may also be humanoid. Tiny fire spirits dance in each candle flame, while mighty salamanders play in desert and volcano. The salamanders also help with invisible combustion, such as our own metabolism, whereby foods are "burnt" to give us energy.

Without Fire there can be no life or light—nothing can be seen. Salamanders are highly intelligent spirits (often much quicker than we are) and one of their functions is to inspire. This is not the inspiration of ideas that comes with the sylphs, but flashes of genius that come when we connect with the Otherworld. Salamanders are also stimulators of passion, including sexual passion, and instill courage, idealism, and vision. Proper contact with the salamanders helps us make good use of our life force, and they also love hearty play, for it renews the soul.

The salamanders are always on the move, and they may be aloof and indifferent to humans at first. They become interested in us when we harness our demons, face ourselves, and meet the challenges of life. Flames are the manifestation of the elemental force, which is Fire. Attune to this and your spirit will ignite.

Dragons

Sadly these wonderful fire spirits have been turned into demons by our culture and its history. They represent unbridled, instinctual power of several types. They personify the fertile, elemental power of Nature and, as such, were regarded as destructive by patriarchal society. This is why there are so many stories about heroes slaying dragons—which, interestingly, are often related to those heroes through family ancestry.

For instance, in Sumerian myth the hero/god Marduk slays the dragon Tiamat, which is actually his own great-great-great-grandmother and from whom he has presumably inherited his power. St. George is another dragon "slayer" and it is worth noting that the name George derives from the Greek *ge*, meaning "earth." Some people have interpreted this as the usurping by men of a power that was essentially female. Others see it as logic and materialism overcoming instinct and the fires of the spirit. The story, as it is given below, is in fact more about courage and common sense.

St. George is the patron saint of England, but he was actually born in Palestine, the son of a Roman officer. In truth he never killed a dragon at all, but rather overcame the irrational fear of it. Here is his story.

In old Beirut the townspeople had, for many years, been terrorized by a dragon that lived in a cave by a stagnant lagoon. When the foul fumes from the lagoon blew over the town, the people would blame the dragon.

It was only a matter of time, they muttered to each other, before the terrible creature came and attacked them. They began to feed it two sheep every day, to keep it at bay. The dragon never came near the town but, not surprisingly, it stayed put, waiting for its regular free lunch. Soon the townspeople ran out of sheep, for they were poor and starving. The dragon was taking all their resources and they were beginning to panic. They turned to the king, beseeching him to save their lives.

"We have given this monster one thousand sheep, and still it will not go away," they cried. "What is to be done?"

The king sat with his head in his hands, and after much thought he made a terrible decision. "We must feed it our children," he told the horrified townspeople. "It is the only way to save our town."

The victims were chosen by a dreadful lottery. Each child was given a number, and each Tuesday a number was drawn and a child was torn from its weeping parents to be tied up outside the dragon's lair. It needed no

noxious vapors from the lagoon to poison the town, for it was filled with horror and sorrow. Faces were pale, and neighbor looked askance at neighbor—no one ever knowing when it would be the turn of his own family to suffer this ghastly fate.

Three months of this had passed, 12 children had been sacrificed and 12 families plunged into mourning when George rode into town. There was great commotion at the palace because, unknown to the king, his own daughter had insisted that she also be given a number and today hers had been pulled out. At that very moment the young princess was tied up outside the dragon's lair, waiting to be devoured by the monster.

"My daughter, my only daughter, my precious golden-haired child," wept the king, struggling to escape from his attendants and save his little girl.

"Your majesty, it is by your own decree, and besides, it is too late. The dragon will have her by now," they told him, some of them secretly pleased that the king would sample the true effects of his decree.

Hearing this, George leapt upon his horse and galloped to where the dragon lurked and the young girl cowered. The townspeople watched from afar, in fear and excitement. When George saw the dragon, he dismounted. Standing between the dragon and the terrified girl, he looked the dragon in the eye. "Your days of eating human flesh are at an end," said George. "Yield to me and your life will be spared."

To the amazement of all who looked on, the great dragon lowered its huge head, as smoke curled from its enormous nostrils.

"Let this foolishness be at an end!" declared George, bowing before the princess, and untying her. "My lady," said he, "I trust you will prove a better sovereign than your father."

Taking a ribbon from the hair of the princess, George bound it round the dragon's neck and led the beast back to the town, along with the joyful girl. Great was the rejoicing in the town, and George was duly rewarded. Several years later the princess married a prince from a neighboring country, and the tame dragon formed part of their wedding procession. However, they were never so foolish as to let it play alone with their children!

WHAT THE STORY MEANS

It is quite obvious that the message of this tale is that the only thing we have to fear is fear itself! It was fear—an unproven fear, at that—that cost the townspeople their sheep, and then (horror of horrors) their children. It was their own stupidity and cowardice that brought sorrow and powerlessness upon them. The dragon in this story merely performed according to their expectations, but once it was confronted, it behaved like a lamb. It is a tough lesson of the fire spirits to face our fears, and to realize that actually they come from nowhere but ourselves.

In myth, dragons often guard treasure. This is symbolic of hidden wisdom that can only be gained through some test of courage or initiative. The dragon, as a truly magical creature, may apparently be slain, but this is a metaphor for overcoming our inner demons and entering the domain of the fire spirits, in an initiation experience that is profoundly changing. Dragons may be regarded as the power that surges within the earth and which sometimes manifest as "ley lines." The Uffington White Horse, carved into the landscape of the English county of Berkshire, is said by some to be a dragon.

In Chinese culture, the dragon is truly valued and is seen as the benevolent, gift-bearing creature that it is. There is a dragon for each of the Elements, and the most powerful of all, the imperial dragon, holds a wonderful pearl either in its claws or under its chin. This magical jewel has the ability to multiply whatever it is placed close to, such as gold, fine clothes, and food.

The dragon has supernatural sight and hearing, and its eyes are often molten gold or shimmering springs. It is a guardian and a tremendous source of spiritual power. If you draw close to one of these

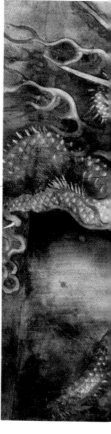

marvelous creatures, it is likely that
your eyes will be opened in some way.
Your strength will increase and you
will be always protected.

Centaurs

Centaurs are half-man and half-horse. They may be included among fire spirits for two reasons. First, the fire sign, Sagittarius, is symbolized by a centaur with a bow and arrow, drawing the centaur into the realms of fiery meanings; second, the centaur is a creature of great power and wisdom, in keeping with other spirits of fire.

Centaurs were originally recognized in Babylonia, where they were guardian spirits. In Greek mythology, the centaurs were wild and unruly, following the wine god, Dionysus, in his revels. Centaurs combine animal passion (in the loins of the stallion) with discrimination (in the human head). The king of the centaurs was called Chiron, and he was a wise and just healer, taught by Apollo.

One day the hero Hercules came to visit the centaurs, and fighting broke out, as it so often did. Chiron tried to calm things down, but to no avail, and in the struggle he was hit in the leg by one of Hercules' poisoned arrows.

Poor Chiron was in agony, but he could not die, for he was immortal. He endured this pain for many a long year, constantly looking for a way to heal himself, but succeeding only in finding better ways to heal others. Eventually a bargain was struck with Zeus, king of the gods. Chiron was to swap his life with that of the titan Prometheus (see page 210) and go to the Underworld in his stead. The centaur gratefully left a world where he had known such suffering, relinquishing his immortality in return for peace.

With their half-human, half-animal characteristics, centaurs bring a change in consciousness, where passion and wisdom can combine. If a centaur should draw close to you, it is possible that new knowledge is rising out of turbulence. Centaurs are great teachers—just as Chiron was—sometimes willing to sacrifice themselves, at other times demandingly selfish. They have a strong sexual energy and may signify the union of masculine and feminine principles, or an actual sexual encounter, with all that means for the inner life. Centaurs are also guardians, and if the strength of one of these beings is working with you, then you will be unstoppable.

Prometheus

In Greek mythology, Prometheus was a titan—a spirit older than the Olympian gods. He was a friend to developing humanity, looking after it and teaching the civilized arts.

Prometheus was also playful, and once he played a trick on Zeus, king of the gods, giving him the bones and gristle of a bull and the meaty parts to hungry people. To punish Prometheus, angry Zeus withheld the gift of fire from humans. So Prometheus crept up to Olympus and stole a spark from the sacred fire.

When Zeus saw fires appearing in hearths all over the earth, he was mad with rage. He chained Prometheus to a mountain rock, and sent an eagle to eat his liver each day. Each night it grew back, and each day the eagle came to eat it again. Such was the dreadful fate of Prometheus, until he was released by Chiron (see page 208).

Prometheus is a fire spirit of courage and idealism. The

"Promethean spirit" is an expression often used for anything innovative, ground-breaking and challenging to established values. Ask Prometheus to inflame you with his spirit—but, unlike him, remember to retain your humility, for always there will be greater powers than those of humans.

Will-o'-the-Wisps

These are strange lights seen hovering over marshland. While they may be attributed to methane gas, science has not fully explained will-o'-the-wisps, and many people believe they are fire fairies, mischievously leading travelers astray, or to safety. Some call them "corpse candles" and say they are an omen of death.

Will-o'-the-wisps are teasing spirits that bring a glimpse of the possible, of adventure, of what we may be. Sometimes the will-o'-the-wisp may remind us of the many little deaths within—deaths of dreams, deaths of hopes, deaths of beliefs. Such "deaths" light up their own "corpse candle," reminding us of what we are losing. Maybe they are dreams that will not die, that have turned into ghosts to haunt us with "what ifs"?

One of the lessons of the fire spirits is that of following our dreams, even if they lead us into danger. In that way we really *live*, rather than simply exist.

Djinn

Djinn, or Genies, are Arabian fairies that are described in the Koran. They are formed of fire, or are the offspring of fire, and in their veins flows flame instead of blood. They are governed by monarchs called Suleyman. In the time before time the Djinn misbehaved, and a legion of angels was sent to put them in their place. A powerful Djinn called Azazel was among the number captured by the angels, and eventually became their king.

W hen Adam was created, the Almighty commanded the angels to worship him, and all complied except Azazel. His name was then changed to Sheytan (that is, "Devil") and he and his followers have remained accursed ever since. This is reminiscent of some Christian attitudes, whereby fairies are seen as allied to evil. Fire fairies simply laugh at this viewpoint!

There are many Djinn of various sizes and powers. The great ones cause the desert sand to swirl upward in a huge, twisting pillar, while lesser ones form dust-devils and other minor manifestations. Like fairies the world over, the Djinn hate iron, for the forging of this metal heralded the end of the rule of Nature and the beginning of the dominion of Man. The Djinn may mate and have families, and while a female Djinn can couple with a man, no mortal female can consort with a male Djinn. They can appear as cats, dogs, or snakes, and lurk in ruins, ovens, and market-places. Sites of commerce attract playful fire spirits, for money can be a powerful energy, for either good or ill. Many Djinn have great magical powers, and the right word can bind them in service to a magician, to whom they may reveal the future.

The Djinn are classic fire spirits who have been denigrated by monotheistic society. It is very convenient for mortal men that they should not have to compete in the love-stakes with a lusty fire demon! These sprites are the possessors of the untameable energy of fire. They know the secrets of the power sources of the Universe and understand the turbulent passions that ignite the human soul. Out of respect they may obey a clever human word, but they are constrained and commanded only at our peril. On a hot day, when the dust swirls and you feel the presence of a Djinn, ask for insight and see what flashes through your brain in the coming moments.

Wayland the Smith

In ancient times the blacksmith was considered to hold magical secrets, for he wielded the transformative power of fire. The only place where it was considered lucky to hang a horseshoe with the horns pointing downwards was over the smithy, thus pouring out magic over the forge.

Wayland was an elf-smith, who made incomparable jewelry. The first part of his story is on page 158, where his swan-maiden wife reclaimed her plumage and left him for the skies. After she left he awaited her return, forging ring after ring to tempt her back to his side. News of his skill and wealth spread, and one night he was ambushed and taken prisoner by Nidud, King of Sweden. Wayland was robbed and set to work making artifacts for the king. The king cut the sinews in Wayland's knees, so that he could not break free.

Imprisoned on Nidud's island, Wayland secretly made a pair of wings from feathers and flotsam that he found on the beach. By his arts he caused the king's daughter to fall in love with him. When the king's two sons went missing, Nidud and his wife assumed they had gone adventuring and consoled themselves with Wayland's latest stunning artifacts, among which were a goblet the size of a human skull, a necklace with four jewels like human eyes, and a glittering brooch made of what looked like 50 gold teeth.

There followed a night of storm, when thunder rolled and lightning ripped the sky. The king and queen were woken by a strange winged figure

me." And so Wayland flew off to find his love, leaving behind him the fruits of his vengeance. The fires of passion in his soul inspired his creativity. Those who tried to imprison him were burnt in the fires of their own greed.

Wayland is an inspiration if you need courage, strength, and perseverance in the face of great obstacles, to find

poised at their window. "Your daughter's love for me has robbed her of her soul," cried a familiar voice. "You, sir, drank from your son's skull; and you, madam, wear your sons' eyes about your neck. The fiery skies await

your heart's desire. Legend tells us that Wayland still dwells in Wayland's Smithy, a barrow-mound near the Uffington White Horse (Berkshire), and that any horse left there overnight will be magically reshod.

Brighid

Brighid also goes by the names of Brigit, Brigid, or Bride (pronounced "Breed"), which means "arrow of fire." She is an ancient Celtic deity, member of the Tuatha de Danann, the magical beings of old Ireland, who became the people of the Sidhe and dwellers within the Hollow Hills (see page 44).

Brighid was daughter of the "Good God," the Dagda, and presided over smithcraft, healing, childbirth, poetry, inspiration, and the Element of Fire. She is also a goddess of the sun, for her symbol is the sun-wheel, which is an off-center cross, symbolizing the cycle of solstices and equinoxes. Some people say that Brighid was actually the Great Mother herself, and that the Dagda was, in fact, her son. Like many ancient deities, she has been denigrated, but has lived on for many centuries in the Christianized version of St. Bridget.

Bridget is reputed to have died about the year 525 CE, but verifiable historical facts about her are thin on the ground, and it would appear that stories of St. Bridget tell of none other than the fairy queen Brighid herself. In one story, Brighid was accused of wickedness by an uncouth man in Ardagh, whereupon she picked up a live coal from a bonfire, placed it in her bosom, and walked with it to the Pound of Killen, suffering no hurt. Where she dropped the coal, a well sprang up, whose waters have been responsible for countless miraculous healings from that day to the present. Brighid is thus in command of the Elements of Fire and Water, and the mistress of healing.

St. Bridget is believed to have been born near Kildare, and it is at Kildare that the fire fairy is remembered. When Pope Gregory the Great decreed that monasteries should be built on pagan sacred sites, the monastery at Kildare was founded. Here there was a shrine to Bridget/Brighid and the nuns tended her sacred flame, never letting it die out, for many a long century.

Glowing Brighid is a goddess whose flame has burnt bright down the centuries. She is one of the easiest fire spirits to call, for it is her nature to heal and to inspire. The simple lighting of a candle and the calling of her name will often bring cheer. If you are suffering from writer's block or need to cleanse and transform your life, the gentle fires of Brighid will work their magic for you.

Finding Fire Fairies

Of all the sprites, fire fairies are the most difficult to encounter. Many of them are not as keen to help humans as other elemental spirits, and they may be disdainful of our slowness. Because of their great mobility they can be hard to attune to. However, wherever there is a sense of play you will find fire fairies, for "play" makes all things possible. They are drawn to any flame, and to strong feelings and creative acts.

Fire fairies ride on the sunbeams, and you may glimpse them wherever a ray pierces through the clouds. They absorb solar energy, which sustains them through the winter. However, the best way to meet the fire spirits is to kindle and tend a fire.

If you have an open hearth, you need look no further, for deep within the glowing embers you will see "fire pictures" that will tell you about the salamanders. Sit before the flames and let yourself feel drowsy and relaxed.

Soon you will be aware of the fire spirits coiling within the glow or dancing in the sparks. If a spark jumps out toward you, that is a fire spirit making its presence felt.

Outside, bonfires are fantastic fire-spirit haunts. Chimeneas (Mexican pottery hearths) and fire-bowls are readily available, and make the creation of fire easy in any garden. Fireworks are the very essence of salamanders, which flock around and within them. Remember to take care when looking for them though.

To make friends with the salamanders, show respect for their Element. Avoid using a microwave—it is an insult! Cook with gas, at the very least, and wherever possible with live coal. Fire sprites appreciate a hearty barbecue! Learn to make fire the old way, by striking wood or using a tinder box, so that you tease the fire from the interior of the wood and the salamanders flash into being. Fire spirits are also attracted by wild and sensuous music. A simple candle is an invitation to them, and tiny sprites dance in each candle flame.

As with all fairies, fire spirits reward interest, respect and a genuine attempt to tune into their way of being. Look for a glint, a flash, a patch of bright color. Maybe a firefly will pass or, at night, your path will be blessed with enchanting glowworms. Fire spirits may also leave gold—anything red, orange, or yellow, or arrow-shaped. Treasure it, and it will light your days.

Making an Altar to the Fire Fairies

Your contact with the salamanders can be affirmed and strengthened
by honoring them on an altar in your home.

METHOD

You will need to set aside a small shelf or similar space as an altar (see page 36).

1 Cover your altar with a cloth of red, orange, or gold, and place on it as many candles as you can, of all shapes and sizes. A combination of red, orange, yellow, and gold candles will look stunning enough to attract the most aloof of salamanders, and you can light them all at once. Needless to say, you should be very careful with all naked flames—even more so if you are consciously trying to attract the fire elementals, for their energies are rampant and uncontrollable!

2 Incense is effective in setting the scene for fire fairies. Choose strong, majestic fragrances, such as frankincense, cedar, cinnamon, coriander, and orange. Basil is said to be good for attracting fire spirits, especially that species of dragon named after it—the basilisk. By all means grow this pungent herb on your fire-fairies altar, in a red pot.

3 Choose some of the many crystals that attract them, such as carnelian, garnet, amber, sunstone, tiger's eye, and red jasper. If you can arrange these so that they catch the light and it glints within them, so much the better.

4 To invoke the help of a specific fire deity, obtain a statue or figurine that seems appropriate. This does not necessarily have to be custom-made. For instance, you may find a statue that represents Bride to you, even though the sculptor had no such image in mind. It is what appeals to you that counts. To attract the healing and heartening energy of this fairy queen into your life, keep a candle—burning safely in a covered lantern—alight there when you are in the house.

5 Dragon figures can be found in all shapes and sizes, some fashioned as candlesticks and joss-stick holders. A horseshoe is considered lucky wherever it is hung, but on or over your fire-fairies altar it is especially symbolic of the transformative powers of fire.

6 To make the atmosphere really crackle, when you need a boost and an influx of salamander energy, light a sparkler or other indoor firework on your altar.

Fire-Spirit Spell for Creativity

Perform this spell when you need an injection of creativity into your heart and life.

METHOD

1 On a sunny day gather four pebbles: a dark one for practicality, a bluish one for clarity, a reddish one for energy, and a green one for serenity. Do this spell in sunlight, or alternatively you could light several yellow, red and/or orange candles.

2 Draw an imaginary circle around you with your fingertip, and visualize it containing all your energies. Place the dark stone (roughly) in the north quarter, the blue in the east, the red in the south, and the green in the west. Starting in the north, imagine all the qualities of concentration and pragmatism entering the pebble from the surrounding light. Face east and imagine all the freedom and clarity of the atmosphere entering that pebble. Now face south and imagine passion

and energy filling the pebble. And lastly face west, drawing peace and calm. Circle clockwise again, face south and feel the energy of light fill your being, so that you are electrified. Ask the salamanders for power.

3 Gather up the pebbles clockwise and place them in a bag. Imagine your circle fading. When you are being creative, take out the pebbles and spread them near you for inspiration.

Fire-Spirit Spell for Success

When you are looking for success—in an exam, interview, or any other venture—try this spell.

METHOD

You will need a red candle; a piece of ginger root and some powdered ginger; a pin; and a red pen and plain paper.

1 Light the candle. Write your purpose on the ginger root, using the pin (you don't have to be too exact!). Spread some powdered ginger on a plate and write your intention in that, too, with a fingertip. For a third time, write your ambition on a piece of paper, with the red pen.

2 Ask the fire spirits to be present, to give their energy to your spell. Imagine them dancing all around you, empowering your ginger.

Burn the paper in the candle flame and, as you do so, imagine succeeding and how happy you will feel. Look at the flame as long as you like, letting yourself daydream about winning.

3 Place a bit of the powdered ginger in your clothing, as appropriate—for instance, if you are running a race, put a little in your sneakers (a tiny pinch will do, or it may irritate your skin). If you are taking an exam, place the ginger root in front of you while you write, for some fire-fairy inspiration.

Meditation to Draw Close to Fire Spirits

The benefits of making contact with the fire spirits are many. They are tremendous energizers, bringers of positive thinking, enthusiasm, and a sense of adventure. Once you have aroused their interest by opening your mind to them, they can be very helpful. They show humans how to moderate the passions within, how to direct and control all strong urges, and how to work with and trust the amazing powers of fire, both in the natural world and on the subtle planes.

METHOD

1 Start your meditation by relaxing completely, as described in the Introduction (see pages 34–35). It is good to do this in sunlight or in front of an open fire. Certainly you need to make sure that you are warm when you do it. Imagine it is a hot, breathless evening, at midsummer. To the west the sky is bathed in brilliant hues of orange, red, and amber. In the east the sky

stars are emerging, twinkling against the purple sky. You are facing south, toward a line of hills, and are standing at the bottom of one of the highest. On the hilltops you see that pyramid-type structures have been erected, and you realize these are beacons—enormous bonfires waiting to be ignited. The air seems electric and, nestling within the undergrowth at your feet, you can see thousands of tiny, glimmering glowworms, like stars come to earth.

2 In the distance, to your left, a shout goes up and one of the beacons flares into life. Another flames in response, and another, and another, until the hilltops stretch into the sunset, blazing in salute to the sky. You realize that you must get closer to all this drama, and so you climb the hill.

3 The air is warm, and although the breeze freshens as you climb, soon the fierce breath of the bonfire envelops you. You feel apprehensive, but you are nearly at the top, almost part of the chain of flame that stretches through the midsummer night. As you arrive on the hilltop plateau, facing the conflagration, you expect to see the other humans responsible for lighting the beacon, but there is no one there to be seen.

4 Mesmerized, you stare into the flames. Within the bonfire all is fluid, incandescent. There are tunnels of flame, walls of flame, turrets of

flame—cities and civilizations seem to come into being and pass away, in the twinkling of an eye. Soon you see forms: here is a serpent, coiling and twisting; there a dragon raising its great head; over there a column of wild horses tossing their fiery manes. Faces come and go, too, laughing, grimacing, and staring. You feel as if you are being given a view of another world, a world of pure energy.

5 Suddenly a shower of sparks erupts from the bonfire and falls around you. These sparks do not dwindle—they grow. You step back, fearing the grass has caught fire, but realize this is a different sort of flame. The grass is not being consumed, and the flames hop and dart from place to place. You watch as each individual spark grows into a capering sprite, made from pure flame. Quick as a flash one of them flies your way. Too late you shrink back, fearing to be burnt. But the sprite flickers around your face and neck and all you feel is a pleasant sense of tickling. You hear a chorus of merry laughter as the sprite leaves you, to dance again with his fellows. You smile too, and begin to relax.

6 Now another spark issues from the fire, falls to the ground before you and grows into a mighty Djinn, taller than you are. Talk to this being. Ask questions, speak of your fears (if you have any) and tell especially of your hopes and dreams, your ambitions and desires. Listen to all the Djinn has to say. You may hear him as a rushing in your ears, or experience him as a feeling of excitement in your heart. Do not be surprised if you suddenly realize you want things you never knew of, or feel drawn to attempt something exceptional. The Djinn can awaken in you powers you never knew you had. Dance with the Djinn, if he wishes, play, and laugh. Know that all things are possible and that the Universe is far, far more mysterious and wonderful than you ever supposed.

7 The time has now come to take your leave, so do so respectfully and with thanks. As you make your way back down the darkened hillside, the salamanders light your way, skipping and shimmering, until you walk through the shadows and find yourself back in everyday awareness. Make a note of your experience.

Meditation to Receive the Gifts of Fire Spirits

Use this meditation to ask the fire spirits to bring the blessings of fire into your life in a way that you will be able to make best use of.

METHOD

1 Begin this meditation in the same way as before (see page 224), approaching the bonfire, meeting the salamanders, and then the Djinn. Ask the Djinn for courage, confidence, the strength to make changes, energy, or inspiration—or ask for all of these things. You may also ask to be shown the future, for fire spirits have the gift of prophecy. However, be aware that the future is not cast in stone. In ancient times people knew they participated in their own destiny, and the very fact of enquiring about the future changed it. When you ask to see your future, it should be in the spirit of "What should I *do?*" rather than "What is going to happen to me?" Fire spirits respect independence.

2 As you ask the Djinn for his help, see how he holds his arms up to the skies, and how flames leap from them into the velvet darkness. The flames form into a ball of fire, which wings its way upward, until it looks like just another star. You watch this star, expecting it to disappear, but see that it is growing again. Something is moving back down toward you, less incandescent than the ball of fire, but bright and flashing. As it draws close to you, you see that it is a magic carpet. The Djinn smiles at you and takes your hand. You feel an electric sensation as his fiery palm touches you—that is all. Guided by him, you leap aboard the magic carpet.

3 Through the warm night you fly, over land and sea. Soon it becomes day, and you see countries and landscapes pass beneath you. Some you recognize, while others look as if they come from another time in history—either the past or the future.

4 Now you are flying over a magnificent city. Its walls flash white, its towers appear to be topped with jewels. The carpet is descending— down, down you go. The air is pleasantly warm, and you see beneath you a temple, the roofs of which are studded with garnets and carnelians, glowing red in the sunshine. On the balcony at the top of the tower someone is softly playing a harp, and the sound echoes around the building.

5 The carpet lands in a lush garden, filled with tropical plants. The Djinn helps you to alight and you follow him toward the temple interior. It is dim within and you enter through an arched doorway. Once inside, your eyes become accustomed to the muted light and you see that the sunlight is filtered through wondrous stained-glass windows. All around you there is a scent of rich incense, frankincense, and cinnamon. Ahead of you, on a large altar, burns a great flame.

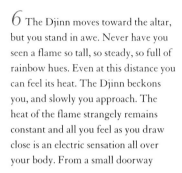

6 The Djinn moves toward the altar, but you stand in awe. Never have you seen a flame so tall, so steady, so full of rainbow hues. Even at this distance you can feel its heat. The Djinn beckons you, and slowly you approach. The heat of the flame strangely remains constant and all you feel as you draw close is an electric sensation all over your body. From a small doorway

beneath the altar, the Djinn takes out a lantern. He opens it, places his own hand in the huge flame and ignites his finger. Then he transfers the flame within the lantern. He looks at you and gives a mighty laugh. "Your gift is here," he says. "Here burns your courage, your wisdom, your energy. Look within and let your soul be set aflame!"

7 You receive the lantern from him, and look at the flame. Stare at this flame for as long as you wish, breathing in the incense smoke, listening to the harp, and feeling the electric air. Draw from the flame the gift you wish for, or look within it for glimpses of the future. Note all that you experience.

8 Now it is time to return. You take your lantern with you, as the Djinn leads you from the temple, through the garden, and back to your carpet. Soon you are whisked through the skies, over city, desert, hill, and vale, until you are back on the midnight hillside, where the beacon burns.

9 Take respectful and thankful leave of the Djinn, and make your way down the hillside, guarding your burning lantern, until your footsteps lead you from that world back into everyday awareness.

10 Light a lantern in this world, as a reminder.

Earth
Fairies

The Element of Earth

Earth is the great nurturer. All that grows and lives draws its substances from the Earth, and everything, when it dies, returns to the Earth, to be transmuted and form the basis of future life.

In some ways earth fairies are *the* fairies that we have all come to picture, from storybooks and tales. These are spirits of tree, flower, stone, and cave. They tend all that lives, and their wisdom is important for our bodies and our lives, for without proper contact with the Element of Earth, we can achieve nothing. Earth contains and gives form, it builds and protects, it holds treasures, and reveals the rhythms of Nature and of our own bodies. In secret, it keeps the seeds until they are ready, by their own special magic, to burst forth. In the same way, our own creativity and artistry depend on a healthy connection with the Earth.

The Earth elemental spirits are called gnomes, and they give special character to every rock, every crystal, and every flowerbed, so these things all have something to teach us, and marvels to reveal. Gnomes are usually attached to a specific place; they do not fly, and their lives are finite. "Gnome" is a generic term for various types of Earth elementals, and by no means all

of them look anything like the little wizened gnomes often shown in books. They create color and texture everywhere and help us attune to the energies of the Earth and tap into its hidden resources.

If we do not have sufficient instinctual contact with the gnomes, we can become "spaced out" and ineffectual. We may neglect our bodies and our health, get lost in "head stuff" or an imaginary world. The gnomes can give us joy in simple things, can adjust our sense of timing and bring us opportunities for real success. They also inspire in us a reverence for all of life, and the ability to balance our own personal interests with those of others, so that we do not become greedy, exploiting, and rapacious.

Of all the elementals, the gnomes have perhaps received the most grievous of hurts, from our abuse of nature and of our own bodies. But they are still there, reliable as ever, proving by their very presence that there are mighty powers within the Earth.

The Leprechaun

The Leprechaun is possibly the most famous of all the earth fairies.
He is an Irish fairy, and few Irish families cannot boast at least one
relative who has, at some time, seen a Leprechaun.

It is well known that Leprechauns are usually clad from head to toe in green. They are solitary male fairies, about 3 ft. (1 m) high. Leprechauns busy themselves making shoes, and are generally none too good-tempered. These fairies have a secret hoard of treasure, and if a human catches a Leprechaun, he or she may be able to persuade him to divulge its whereabouts; but if that human should take his eyes off the fairy for even a split second, the Leprechaun will disappear, along with his gold. This is the story of how Seamus met his own Leprechaun.

Seamus was a good lad, hard-working and honest. He was also clever and loved to read books, but because his family was poor, there had never been enough money to educate him. Still, Seamus consoled himself with stories and poetry, philosophy and history, dreaming of the day when he would be able to go to the big town, with its graceful spires that reached the sky, and study at the university there.

One hot midsummer evening, Seamus was returning home from the fields, his shovel over his shoulder and a book under his arm, when he heard a tapping sound coming from behind the hedge that lined his path. Seamus quietly put down what he was carrying and tiptoed towards the sound. Carefully parting the bushes, he spied a little man, clad in green, hammering away at the sole of a tiny shoe.

Naturally Seamus knew all about Leprechauns, and he was well aware of

what he needed to do. Quick as a flash he grabbed the little man by his arm and held him in a vice-like grip as he struggled to be free.

"I'll not be lettin' you go, now, until you tell me where it is you have your store of gold," said Seamus.

"Ah, you're chokin' me—for pity's sake!" cried the Leprechaun. Seamus felt ashamed of his roughness and gently set the little man on the ground, being careful not to take his eyes off him. The Leprechaun coughed, straightened his green waistcoat and gave a little bow in the direction of Seamus. "You're a kind young fella," said the fairy. "Tell me why, now, you're so anxious to get your hands on me pot of gold! Are you greedy, or needy, that's the question?"

Seamus told the little man all about his poverty, his life of toil, and his dreams. All the while he was careful not to take his eyes off the Leprechaun. The sprite eyed him closely, as if weighing him up.

"Well, well—I believe you, so I do," said the Leprechaun. "And so I'm thinkin' that I'll be showin' you me store of gold."

With these words and a quick sideways glance, the little man took off through the fields, running like a hare, with Seamus—who was luckily very fit—hot on his heels. Many times Seamus stumbled, for he could not look where he was putting his feet for fear of losing sight of the Leprechaun. At length, exhausted, the little man stopped by a barrow-mound, on which lay a very large rugged boulder.

"There you go," panted the little man. "You'll find me treasure if you creep through the crack in that rock. But mind now, you'd best be hurryin'! If the sun sets on you, you'll be trapped in the rock for all eternity!"

With his eyes still fixed on the Leprechaun, Seamus followed him through the narrow crack into the hollow hill. There, glinting in the darkness, was a huge pot spilling over with gold coins. "Riches—I am made

for life!" exclaimed the young man, stuffing his pockets full of coins and trying to lift the pot.

"Much good it'll do you if you're stuck here for life!" said the fairy. "Sunset is but a moment away."

Seamus tried once more to lift the pot, realized it was impossible, grabbed as many coins as he could and launched himself through the crack just as the sun dipped below the horizon and the barrow-mound was plunged into shadow. He heard the stone close behind him, and when he turned, there was no crack to be seen and no sign of the Leprechaun.

Seamus hurried home, holding his treasure in his coat. His family was overjoyed to see him and soon they were all living in a fine house, with a carriage and servants. Seamus was able to study at university, and some years later he was a famous writer, loved throughout Ireland for the wonderful stories he told. But he never forgot the little man who had made all this possible—and his pockets were always full of fairy gold!

WHAT THE STORY MEANS

It isn't hard to pick out many meanings in this story. In the first place it shows how the earth, and the spirits that are part of her, provide in the case of genuine need. Seamus shows enterprise and determination. He is also kind—not everything comes second to his wishes, for he has mercy on the little man when he seems to be strangling him. For this the sprite decides to trust and reward him. But Seamus also has a healthy sense of self-preservation and plenty of ambition and determination. Having found the Leprechaun, there is no way he is going to let him out of his sight. One message of the earth fairies is that we must be aware of our own legitimate needs and be prepared to prioritize them—we need to take practical action in order to realize our goals.

Seamus also has good judgement. He knows that if he is quick enough, he can get into the fairy fort and out again before sundown. He trusts his own abilities, and the skills and strengths of his own body.

Above all, Seamus is not greedy. Tempted by all that shining gold, many men might have been unable to leave any behind, and so would have been caught beneath the earth for the rest of their lives. Seamus has the sense to realize that he must moderate his winnings if he is to enjoy any of it and for this he is rewarded.

The story is an illustration of the balance that can exist between humans and the earth. There is enough for all to enjoy, if we are fair, considerate, and moderate. The fairies don't think that is too much to ask!

Dwarfs

From Iceland to the Indian subcontinent, dwarfs were traditionally
fairies that lived within the earth and mined its treasures to shape into
beautiful artifacts.

The Icelandic body of lore known as the Eddas describes how the gods of old formed the world from the dismembered body of the giant Ymir. As they did so, maggots fell from his putrefying flesh and became the dwarfs. To these the gods gave great strength and intelligence, and sent them to dwell below the earth. The dwarfs have magical stones that give them wisdom, and the power to make themselves invisible. They guard the resources of the earth, especially minerals, and haunt caves and mines, rather like the Knockers (see page 244).

Favorite haunts of dwarfs are mountain regions, and they can also move with ease through the earth. They are short of stature, their skin is gray and they look very old and gnarled. Often they hide their feet, for they may look like those of a crow or goose or may point backward. These beings may not be seen by day, for one ray of sun turns them into stone. The dwarfs are somewhat sad, for there are no females, and new dwarfs have to be fashioned by them out of the living rock. Perhaps because of this they are reputed to steal human babies, leaving in place of the child a changeling, which may be a little wizened dwarf.

Dwarfs can be helpful to humans, lending them artifacts for celebrations, although most of their kind have now moved away from civilization and are seen no more. The dwarfs also helped the gods. In one Norse tale, the trickster god Loki cut off all the lovely golden hair of the goddess Sif while she

new hair, from pure gold, able to take root within the head of Sif and grow again. So Loki was spared, to perform further mischief in the days to come.

These days the dwarfs may be hard to spot, but they will help if you ask them. When you need

was sleeping. Her husband, the mighty thunder god Thor, was ferociously angry, and Loki fled to the dwarfs for help. So clever were they that they spun all your resourcefulness to get out of a tight spot, the dwarfs will whisper their inspiration and lend a deft touch to your hand.

Knockers

Knockers were active in the days of the Cornish tin mines. They were friendly to the miners, for they knocked to let them know where the richest veins of ore might be found. Generally Knockers only made themselves known through sound, but miners would also report seeing them—little imps, sitting on pieces of wood or performing funny antics.

These fairies are also called Buccas, Gathorns, Spriggans, Nickers, and Nuggies. They are occupied with the affairs of the earth and may be doing their own kind of mining.

Although generally benevolent, like all fairies Knockers can be offended, and they do not like swearing or whistling. They are not keen on anything that is shaped like a cross, and so miners were very careful not to mark this on anything. A dislike for the cross does not arise from satanic associations, but possibly from the fact that all fairies know that Christianity has demonized them—so they tend to get offended! The equal-armed cross is also a powerful symbol of the material world and the four points of the compass. Earth spirits may well feel that this is *their* special sign.

In the English West Country, there are many tales about the Knockers. One concerns Ransom Mine, where so much knocking was heard that all were convinced this must be a very rich mine, yet the miners were all too afraid to work, because of the Knockers. Eventually one old man who had something of "the sight" went out at midnight, at midsummer, along with his son, and watched until he saw the fairies bringing up the ore. A bargain was struck with them whereby the father and son would work the ore for the fairies and would always leave them one-tenth of the best, for their own use. After this, the old man and his son became very wealthy, and the old man never failed to leave the fairies their due, as promised. Sadly, after his death his son grew greedy. He cheated the fairies and so they stopped cooperating with him. No more ore came from the mine and he wasted all his father's legacy on drink, dying a penniless beggar.

Why do so many humans take the riches of the earth—both within mines and upon the surface—for granted? And why can we not see that, in cheating the powers of life, we only cheat ourselves? There is enough for all and joy in sharing.

Cerridwen

Cerridwen is a Welsh hag fairy and Underworld goddess, who had the power of transformation and fertility. The sow is one of her symbols, because it is so fertile.

S he had a daughter named Creirwy, the most beautiful girl in the world, and a son named Afagddu, which means "darkness." So ugly was this boy that Cerridwen wished to compensate him, and so she brewed a magic potion in her cauldron, which would confer wisdom and inspiration on the unfortunate lad. This potion had to brew for a year and a day, so Cerridwen enlisted the help of a boy called Gwion, to help her stir it.

One day, while Cerridwen was out gathering herbs to add to the cauldron, Gwion grew tired and his head began to nod. As he jerked awake, the great ladle flipped and a drop of the scalding liquid landed on his thumb. He sucked it, to alleviate the pain, and instantly became the possessor of ultimate knowledge, intended for Afagddu. When Cerridwen came back, Gwion tried to hide, but the fairy sensed what had happened and she was furious. She pursued him relentlessly. He changed into a hare and fled, so she became a greyhound; he became a fish, and she an otter; he became a bird, and she turned into a hawk. Finally he became a grain of corn, but she turned into a hen and ate him. Nine months later Cerridwen gave birth to Taliesin, the greatest of all bards.

This story is often interpreted as a tale of initiation. Gwion and Cerridwen pass through all four Elements: Fire as the swift-moving greyhound and hare, Water as the fish, Air as the birds, and Earth as the hen and corn. This means being inwardly transformed by deep experiences, which is one of the gifts of the fairy realm. This may in turn give rise to wonderful creativity, as with Taliesin.

Cerridwen represents the deep power of the earth, which changes all things in time. It is the tomb, where all go when they die, yet it is also the womb, from which all things grow. The earth holds the mystery of life and death, for life depends on death, just as death follows life, in due cycle. The shape-shifting story of Cerridwen also represents the cycle of the seasons, in which all is transformed. This dark goddess holds the key to the wisdom of the Underworld, which is beyond words.

Pan of the Goat's Feet

Pan is an ancient god of shepherds and pasture. His name means "all," suggesting that he embodies the mute forces of the earth. The word "panic" derives from it, and panic can come upon us when we are alone in the wild, aware of the vastness of Nature. Pan has the feet of a goat, animal legs, a human torso, and a horned head, combining many levels of life in his person.

In old Arcadia, Pan fell in love with a beautiful nymph, Syrinx, but she spurned him. At first Pan did not take this seriously—so many of the nymphs had run from him, but never too fast, and eventually he had his way with them all. Laughing, he pursued her. However, Syrinx was running like the wind and he could hear her voice, whimpering and crying. They were coming to a river, and Syrinx was trapped. Normally at this point Pan would have pounced on the giggling nymph, but Syrinx was distressed— puzzled, Pan watched as she raised her arms in the air and implored the other gods for help.

Pan was a lusty god, and his appeal had never failed him in the past. Surely if he did not frighten Syrinx, she would understand what pleasure he could give her and would melt into his arms! Slowly he approached her, but as he drew close, her form changed, so that he could see the river through her. The lovely nymph had turned into a clump of reeds that shivered in the breeze.

Pan sat forlornly by the river, listening to the strange and mournful sound of the wind in the reeds. Then

he had an idea. His love might be gone from him, but he could still make music. Carefully he plucked some of the best reeds and bound them together with grass, to make his panpipes. He walked off slowly through the forest, playing the poignant strains that have become his hallmark.

When you are on your own beside some lonely river bank, or wandering on a hillside, listen for the pipes of Pan on the breeze, for they are the very breath of wildness. However, Pan is no mere love-crossed minstrel—he is a creative pragmatist who knows how to make the best of a bad job. If you feel thwarted, he can show you how to turn failure into success and move forward.

Pixies and Piskies

Pixies are found in the English West Country (the counties of Cornwall, Devon, and Somerset), while Piskies are purely Cornish. These are two different names for what is essentially the same kind of sprite.

Belief in piskies was once total, and every house would have a "pisky pow" on the ridge-tiles of the roof, so that these fairies had somewhere to dance. Their favorite haunts are the prehistoric sites that abound in the West Country, around standing stones or along the banks of rivers, and they live in fairy mounds. Piskies wear white waistcoats and green stockings, with shoes that are polished until they gleam. Pixies are little green creatures, who wear bells that can often be heard tinkling over hill and dale as they dance. Dartmoor pixies may ride the wild ponies, teasing them and knotting their manes. Some say they can also turn into hedgehogs.

Some believe that these fairies are the souls of the prehistoric peoples of England, and that they are getting smaller and smaller, until eventually they will disappear completely. This is reminiscent of the Irish people of the Sidhe. True, these beings may disappear from sight, but that is only because we—with our "scientistic" outlook—have ceased to be able to see them, not because they are gone.

Pixies love to lead travelers astray, and there are many tales of wanderers being lost for many days in forest and moor. One Devonshire farmer could not find the way out of his own field, until he remembered how to fox the fairies. He took off his coat and turned it inside out, whereupon the pixies flew away into the trees, laughing at him. Another story tells of a boy from St. Allen, near Truro in Cornwall, who went missing while gathering wild flowers in the woods. For three days his distraught family sought him, only to find him asleep in the same copse where he had vanished. He told how he had followed the sound of wonderful birdsong into the forest, as night fell. The stars came out, and each one was a pixie. They took him to a jeweled cave, fed him honey, and sang to him. He fell asleep, and awoke in the copse.

Like brownies, pixies can also help humans, by threshing corn and the like. Pixies are there to help us learn not to take life too seriously. Laughter is wonderful medicine, and the earth is a healing force.

Gwyn ap Nudd

Gwyn is the Welsh King of the Underworld, ruling the fair Welsh fairies, called the Tylwyth Teg. These are beautiful but tricky creatures, who guard their domain in the earth jealously. Gwyn also leads the cavalcade of spirits called the Wild Hunt into his domain beneath Glastonbury Tor in Somerset (see page 91).

Much poetry has been written about Gwyn, for he is a hero who battles with his counterpart Gwythyr each May Day for the hand of the fairy maiden Crieddyled. Legend tells how Crieddyled married her lover Gwythyr, but Gwyn abducted her before the marriage could be consummated. This is a very ancient tale about the powers of light and dark, winter and summer, which must battle each spring and autumn for the hand of the earth goddess. The goddess may appear passive in this, but really she possesses the deep wisdom to know that there is a season for everything and, while battles are won and lost, she and her cycles continue. Gwyn and Gwythyr must fight each other each year, until the end of time.

Another story tells how Gwyn summoned St. Collen to meet him at the top of the Tor, after Collen had made an objection to him being called the lord of the Underworld. Reluctantly the saint went to the rendezvous, taking with him a flask of holy water. There on the Tor was a marvelous castle, surrounded by beautiful maidens and handsome youths, dancing to the sound of minstrels, and feasting. In the center sat Gwyn, on a throne of gold. He invited the saint to partake of some of the food, but Collen refused and instead threw the holy water over Gwyn, whereupon the entire company and the castle disappeared, leaving St. Collen alone on the windswept Tor.

Despite being offended by holy water, Gwyn is still with us, for he is a spirit of the seasonal cycle that must go on inexorably, while the world turns, until the time of humans comes to an end. When we need the courage to face the inevitable, to go through transformations and walk through whatever part of the Underworld calls to us, Gwyn can strengthen our hearts and let us know that, however bad things look, the wheel will inevitably turn in our direction once more, and we will triumph.

The Green Man

The term "The Green Man" is actually very new, for it was coined by the author Kathleen Basford, in her book of the same name, in 1978. However, the spirit of the Green Man is as ancient as the primeval forests that once covered the earth.

The Green Man is usually seen sculpted as a foliate mask—that is, a face made from leaves. He may appear as a human head surrounded by leaves, or the leaves may make up the face. Even more wild-looking, vegetation may be seen coming out of his mouth. Sculptures of the Green Man can be found in countless churches in Britain and Europe, and as far apart as Moscow and New Delhi. He may be carved in stone or wood, or be shown in a stained-glass window. More recently the Green Man image has appeared on public buildings, inns, walls, benches, and in private homes. The Green Man spirit is also enacted in many local customs, such as the Hastings May Day Jack-in-the-Green procession, which was revived by the Mad Jacks Morris Dancers in 1979.

But what of the true Green Man? He can be glimpsed wherever there is vegetation—he is one of the easiest spirits to contact. Wherever there is greenery, he is present. He has countless faces, and often his face may change while you are looking at it. You may see this countenance when you look at the gnarled bark of an ancient tree, or when you gaze into a curtain of green leaves. Just let your eyes go slightly glazed, focusing beyond what you are actually looking at, and the Green Man will appear in all his wildness and wisdom.

The Green Man is the quintessence of growth. He is very powerful, for he is the unstoppable urge of life to perpetuate itself. So strong is this that green shoots will even pierce through concrete, seeking the light, proving that Mother Earth has dominion. The Green Man is her emissary.

There are Green Women, too, and these may also be found carved in churches. The Green Woman is more of a dryad spirit, which is covered in the section on Tree Fairies (see page 339). There is a gentler aura to these spirits, although they can be fierce in protecting their trees.

A Green Man mask can be bought in many garden centres and New Age shops. Let this image inspire you, with strength and faith in Nature.

Cernunnos

Cernunnos is the horned god of the Wildwood. He is
the protector of all the forest creatures, yet he is also
the hunter. He embodies the cycle of life, which
involves growth and nurture, but also death
and destruction. His antlers proclaim
strength, vitality, and an earthy endurance.

Cernunnos is a very mysterious and ambiguous figure, for his message is that both hunted and hunter are in fact one, in the spiral of life. It is probable that in the days of the hunter-gatherers, the figure of Cernunnos was invoked regularly (although by a different name) by hunters who wished to identify with their prey. This was not just about learning how to catch the animal, but also about honoring and respecting it, and acknowledging dependence on it, as the Native Americans do on the buffalo. It was also about realizing that the hunter will inevitably one day be hunted, by his own death, and will return his bones to the earth, to nourish new life.

Cernunnos may also be called Herne. He may appear as a horned figure, in the mist, or as a stag. If you see him, then you may be being called to explore your own mysticism and the deeper meanings of life.

Robin Hood

Robin is known as one of the greatest legendary figures in British folklore, but stories about him may well have arisen from a non-human source: Robin Hood, the outlaw, lived in the Greenwood, wore green and (like many elves) shot dangerous arrows; Robin Goodfellow is a puckish type of sprite, which may behave like a pixie. The Robin legends are probably a conflation of both stories.

Robin is a nature god and, like all earth spirits, despises greed and fights evil. Respect the forest and Robin will be your guide on the Greenwood paths. His mischief is there to restore our sense of value, and he also brings the gift of sensuous joy in the richness of life.

Robin's arrows may suggest a flight of the mind, and arrows are often associated with the spirit world. Stone Age flint arrow-heads were often called "elf-bolts" and are most likely to be found near fairy mounds. It is very lucky to discover one.

Giants

Giants have been a part of many creation myths. It is often assumed that fairies are small, but that is by no means necessarily the case, and giants are truly part of the fairy realm.

These beings are embodiments of the primal forces of an area of the natural world, guarding the treasures of Mother Nature. There are mountain giants, forest giants, and river giants, and they hold wisdom and power. Their energies tend to magnify those of humans, so they may appear scary to anyone who is not well intentioned, reflecting back at them their own evil.

Creatures such as the Yeti (Abominable Snowman) and Bigfoot are such fairies, and they are very difficult to encounter as they are the living breath of their environment and shape-shift within it, or become invisible. Their footprints indicate that there are things in this world much larger than we can comprehend. Giants remind us to be humble; indeed, they champion the common folk and uphold the nobility of leading a good and natural life, in harmony with all that surrounds us.

The message of giants is that things need to be brought into proper perspective. They hold inspiration about how we can become greater than we are, stronger and more effectual. These creatures may also be protecting some special area or growing thing. They may be drawn to the vulnerable, the weak, the timid, or to those who are innocent and child-like. Giants often look after that which is not properly valued, as if their size was trying to indicate, "This *is* important!"

If you have an encounter with a giant, it may well be that there is a personal message there for you. What is it that is bang-smack in front of your nose that you are not seeing? What plain fact or practical matter needs your attention, while you are off thinking about less important things? The giant may have a symbolic meaning for you—for instance, one carrying a club may be calling you to develop your inner strength; or one such as Bigfoot may be reminding you to recall your animal instincts. Do not fear giants, for they may amplify your fear and send it back to you, whereas if you send them love and consideration, you will be gifted with the same many times over.

Drawing Close to Earth Fairies

We have a much-neglected hotline to the gnomes in our own bodies. Instead of treating our bodies as temples to our souls, we abuse them in all manner of ways and shove synthetic substances into them, expecting them to cope. With the help of the gnomes, they usually do, but our lack of respect ultimately causes grievous harm to our physical health, and to our instinctual link with the earth and the nature-spirit realm.

A good way to attract the gnomes initially, and to flag up to them that we are attuning to their presence, is to respect our bodily needs and to eat natural, unrefined fresh produce from local sources. It is also best to cleanse ourselves of drugs, including alcohol, nicotine, and caffeine. This does not mean undergoing a fanatical detox, but simply a return to basics. Everything on the earth—even the most synthetic substance—is "natural," for it came originally from the earth. However, some things have been so short-sightedly and disrespectfully distorted by humans that no self-respecting gnome would come within half a mile of them!

In respect of drugs, it is true that shamans in native cultures often take drugs made from plants, and thus have profound contact with the plant-spirit. However, that is very different from the recreational use of drugs, which can open the portals in a careless, uncontrolled, and dangerous manner.

Attend to the practicalities of your life, consciously and deliberately, enjoying the solid contact you are making with *things*. Do some housework, make cakes and bread, sew, mend, make wine or beer, do woodwork or home repairs—above all, tend the garden, if you have one; if you do not, take special care of your house plants. Concentrate too on your financial affairs, not in order to speculate, or to be miserly, but just to know where you stand.

Try to feel in contact with your physical self, your strength, your bodily sensations, your health, and sexual energies, for all such are grounding, earth-spirit matters. Use all the practical talents you have, such as music or painting, and be generous with others in due measure. Adopt a sensible routine—not to be imprisoned by it, but because this actually sets you free to think about other things. The gnomes understand that to be free of worry about material things, we have to follow the rules of the Earth— and then everything falls into place.

Making an Altar to the Earth Fairies

Earth fairies love their familiar spots, and with any luck there will be some close to you already. You can intensify this connection by creating a devotional space in their honor.

METHOD

You will need to set aside a small shelf or similar as a special altar to the earth fairies (see page 36).

1 It is sometimes possible to find brown candles, so get these if you can for your altar. Failing this, bright green or a dusky gold will be suitable. Incense or joss-sticks of an earthy fragrance, such as patchouli, honeysuckle, or vervain, will also strike the right note. Cover the altar in a brown or vibrant green cloth, if this appeals to you.

2 While different crystals have links with various Elements, Earth is powerful in this respect, and earth spirits have a strong connection with many crystals; they were closely involved in their formation, and will be drawn in an attitude of cooperation and protection to the spirit within the crystal, with which they can work. So place on your altar a profusion of crystals, choosing any that appeal to you, in the knowledge that the earth fairies will approve. Crystals such as moss agate, onyx, jet, amber, brown jasper, and peridot are particular earthy favorites.

3 By all means swathe your altar in cut greenery, such as ivy. This grows well and can easily be replenished. But remember that the earth sprites love plants that are actually growing and will be drawn to those needing their attention. So place small pots of primroses or herbs in among your crystals. You can also gather stones when you are out walking, and build a small cairn for the earth fairies.

4 If you wish to attract a specific spirit, look out for symbols and figurines that represent him or her, and give pride of place to these on your altar. The Green Man is easily come by, and will bring the ancient forest close to your home. If you want to attract money, what better symbol than a little Leprechaun? Cernunnos can be invoked using a stag figure, and Cerridwen using a cauldron. Earth fairies will be impressed by practical attention to their sacred space, preferably in a sensible routine, so make sure that you cleanse, tidy and freshen it at regular intervals, and you will be enriched.

Finding Earth Spirits in the Wild

Earth spirits are just about the easiest ones to make contact with. Their forms tend to be less subtle than those of many fairies, and they generally stick to one place—so if you feel a location is haunted by these beings, it will always be haunted. Wherever anything grows, there will be a fairy to attend to it.

Earth fairies love gardens, and will gather round you while you are planting and watering. At the end of a hot day they exult when you get out the hose or watering can, and will dance among the refreshed flowers with glee. Often they do not like you weeding, though, so make sure you always do this with respect. Leave a patch of your garden to grow wild, for the fairies love this and it creates a space for all the plants that are unwelcome elsewhere—just because humans do not like them, this does not mean they do not have a valuable place in the scheme of things.

METHOD

1 To draw close to the gnomes, settle quietly in your garden or in a park, woodland, field, or hillside—close to a barrow-mound may be the most powerful place of all. Gnomes of the deep earth may be experienced in a cave or hollow, whereas others may be more of the flower- or tree-fairy types, which have their own sections in this book (see pages 299 and 337). Let your bare feet and hands make contact with the earth, mud, or stone. Beat a soft rhythm on a drum, if you wish.

2 Be very still, relaxed, and quiet. Try not to see anything, because that will put you in the wrong frame of mind. Just be there, and be observant—these spirits do not show themselves in the ways you might expect, and seeing them can seem almost ordinary.

3 Be aware of any little movements out of the corner of your eye, for that is where spirits are often first perceived. An animal running in the undergrowth may also be a shy gnome in disguise. Look out for the face of the Green Man among the leaves, and watch flowers, for they can also be sweet faces, nodding and smiling.

4 To show they have drawn close to you, gnomes will often give you a tangible gift, such as a coin or a piece of jewelry. If you find this on your path, treasure it, for it is very lucky.

Earth-Spirit Spell for Money

Money is energy and power. It is good to ask for this and to use it wisely. The gnomes can bring you strength and common sense to enrich you, along with that little bit of luck, to give you the edge.

METHOD

You will need some nuts, on which you should inscribe roughly with a pin the amount of money you want (in multiples of ten, to make up your total); you also need a green candle, a green pen, and some paper.

1 Arrange the nuts around the candle. Light the candle and imagine the gnomes drawing close. Ask them to open up ways for you to make this money. Clearly imagine the money arriving—you do not have to be specific about how it does so. Pledge a gift for the earth in return.

2 Eat the nuts slowly and deliberately, still imagining the sum of money arriving. Then take the pen and a piece of paper the size of a cheque. Write yourself a cheque for the amount that you require.

3 Put this somewhere safe, and carry on doing your best to earn money. The sum may come from several sources. Remember to thank the gnomes when it does, and give back your promised gift in return.

Earth-Spirit Spell for Achievement

Do this spell when you need to feel a sense of achievement in any task that you are performing.

METHOD

You will need a brown or green candle; some compost, a seed tray, and some seeds (cress seeds are easy to grow); plus a symbol of the thing you wish to achieve—such as a ring for a relationship, a key for a home, and so on.

Relight your candle from time to time, and again ask the gnomes for their help.

1 Light the candle and spread the compost in the seed tray. Press your symbol beneath the soil in the tray. Ask the gnomes to help you "plant" your desire firmly and securely.

2 Now sow the seeds according to the instructions, asking the gnomes to help them take root and grow. Place them in an appropriate place to germinate.

3 When the seeds grow, water them carefully and tend them. Affirm that, as they grow, so your wish is coming into being. Don't worry if the seeds do not grow—it simply means you need to do the spell again and ask the gnomes really nicely. The great thing about this spell is that you will feel your connection with the earth spirits grow, along with your germinating seeds.

Meditation to Make Contact with the Earth Spirits

Do this meditation outside, if you can find a quiet spot. All the
natural scents and sounds will intensify your experience. However,
it is very important that you should not be disturbed.

METHOD

1 Start by relaxing completely, as described in the Introduction (see pages 34–35). Close your eyes and either imagine the actual place where you are sitting/lying or that you are somewhere else in Nature. Take the time to see this in detail. If you are using the place where you are, do not be surprised if it changes in some way.

2 Around you there are soft sounds of rustling and scuffling. The undergrowth seems to be moving here and there, this way and that, as if there are creatures within it. Each time you turn round to get a better look, the movement seems to stop. You feel that you are being watched by curious eyes.

3 The vegetation around you is becoming indistinct. You realize a soft gray mist is rising from the ground, slowly obscuring all that you see. Up, up goes the mist, around and above you, until you find yourself in a bell jar of whiteness. Peace surrounds you, and you wait patiently.

4 Now the mist is clearing in front of you, revealing a different scene entirely. You see there is a forest path, dark and over-arched by thick branches, winding deep into the heart of the woodland. You know that you must take this path.

earth beneath your feet is springy and even, although the forest grows thick on both sides. As you walk, you are aware that the undergrowth on either side of the path is moving from time to time. Gradually you realize that beings are walking alongside you. As you walk on, they become clearer and clearer, until you can see their faces and fairy forms.

6 Ahead you can see a dark shape looming. The earthy scent intensifies, and you realize you are approaching the mouth of a cave. You stand before it, and the beings on either side of you stand still too. Beside the path there is a flat stone. You sit on it and wait.

7 You are becoming aware of a rhythmic sound, like a heartbeat or a muffled drum. The noise is steadily getting louder, and you realize that it is the sound of footsteps approaching. You feel a little apprehensive, but notice that all your companion earth spirits are clustering expectantly at the mouth of the cave, so you also watch patiently and hopefully.

5 You get up and begin to walk into the tunnel of green. Bird calls echo overhead. The air is still and cool, and there is a scent of moss and soil. The

8 The sound intensifies to a steady boom, until a figure appears in the shadowed arch of the cave. This is a mighty creature, which looks as if he has been hewn from solid rock: gnarled, gray-brown, and sinewy. His feet are like tree roots and his arms like the branches of an oak, and he carries a great club over his shoulder. For a moment you feel afraid, until you notice that above his tangled beard his eyes are brown and twinkling.

9 This being squats down, and as he does so he looks much more homely. All the gnomes and nature spirits throng around him and he laughs a deep, booming laugh as they climb upon his knees and shoulders and whisper in his ear. All the while he looks sidelong at you, winking and nodding, until you approach a little closer. "Look around you," he says, and his voice is surprisingly soft, like the rain falling on thirsty ground. "Look around, listen around, *feel* around!" You look about you, into the green and fertile forest. "Here," he says, "is where it all happens. Do you understand? All takes shape, you take shape, everything is."

10 Thoughts rise in your mind and feelings within your heart. Ask questions of the Gnome King. Speak to him especially of your plans and ambitions, your practical difficulties, and matters to do with your home, money, and body. Ask how you can proceed in love and harmony with the earth, while finding fulfillment. Don't be surprised if some of his answers are quite short and to the point.

11 Soon the time comes to take your leave. Do so respectfully and thankfully. Walk back along the forest path, with such of the earth spirits as have chosen to accompany you. As you approach the place where you began, see that the mist has disappeared and all is normal. Come back gradually to everyday awareness.

Meditation to Receive the Gifts of Earth Spirits

Perform this meditation to receive the Gnome King's gifts, for they are plentiful, but seek him also for his wisdom, for it is as rich as the earth herself.

METHOD

1 Begin in the same way as before (see page 268) to meet the earth spirits. Walk down the forest path to the entrance to the cave. Listen for the booming footsteps of the Gnome King.

2 He stands in the dark archway and, with his gnarled finger, beckons you. You follow him into the cave, where a subtle glow is emanating from the rocks. Every so often the Gnome King turns round to see if you are following, and you are sure his lips twitch into a mischievous smile.

3 On and on you walk, steadily downward, with the cave always curving, so that if you do not keep up with the Gnome King you will lose sight of him.

4 Eventually the ground widens into a magnificent cavern. The roof is too high to see, but there appear to be stars caught upon it, for you glimpse a twinkling in the darkness. Here there are many beings similar to your guide, working raw stone into shapes or hammering in adjacent chambers, where you see the glint of flames. In the center of the cavern is an awesome pile of precious and semi-precious stones, shining in many colors.

5 The Gnome King beckons, and you approach this pile. He draws forth a huge emerald that fills his massive palm and becomes perfectly rounded: it is an exact replica of the earth, the continents, and the seas, in exquisite miniature. The Gnome King holds out the globe towards you. "See what you and your kind are doing," he says.

6 You gaze at the globe and it feels as if you are being drawn within it. You see forests being cut down, land polluted by pesticides and depleted by intense farming; oceans poisoned, habitats destroyed, species rendered extinct; and the suffering of humans whose lands are disappearing or who are starving due to the greed of others. You begin to feel distressed, but sense a huge, warm hand on your shoulder. "When will your kind learn that there is enough for all?" the Gnome King asks. "When will you understand that what you give comes back to you? I will give you a gift now, for I know it will come back to the earth through you, who are learning to cherish her."

7 He draws a wonderful crystal from the shining pile and gives it to you. "Take this back to your own world," he says. "Make of it what you want, for it can turn into the desire of your heart, as long as your heart is open, generous, and loving."

8 You take your crystal and the Gnome King leads you out of the chamber, upward through the earth to the cave entrance. There you take your leave, reverently and thankfully. Walk back along the forest path and come slowly back to everyday awareness. What will you make of your jewel? Enjoy it! And what will you give? Enjoy that, too, and visit the Gnome King again from time to time.

House
and Hearth
Fairies

Fairies in the Home

A home is very special. It is a place of growth, nurture, care, and protection, where love and life are affirmed. This is much more than simply a place to stay. In a home there is a special ambience that surrounds you, just as much as the four walls.

A true home does not comprise solely bricks and mortar, but also exists on the subtle planes, where it is a center for certain energies. Spirits are attracted to a home, and these may be helpful, although sometimes they are mischievous and playful.

Some houses may be situated on ley lines, or what are believed to be lines of power within the earth. Such homes will be more subject to all manner of psychic phenomena, and may have quite a strong "atmosphere." Hauntings and poltergeist phenomena may be common there. The dividing line between ghosts, poltergeists, and fairies is always a thin one.

Any home that is loved has an atmosphere that attracts sprites, and these will help to make that atmosphere stronger and more appealing. Fairies take up residence in houseplants, helping them to grow and even giving you reminders to tend and water them by making movements as you pass, which you catch out of the corner of your eye. Then you say to yourself, "Ah, I must attend to that plant now!"

Fairies also love kitchen activity, and will help bread and cakes to rise, as if by "magic." In some places food seems to remain good long after its "use by" date, due to the freshness imparted by domestic "little people." A home that is blessed with fairy helpers always seems light and bright, the air there feeling fresh, with a hard-to-identify fragrance. Fairies hate dirt, and will often help, in their subtle way, to minimize dust in a home they love. However, they do enjoy a mischievous swing on a cobweb! Try to show

your respect for life by never killing spiders or insects, and with luck the fairies will reward you by keeping them at bay.

Needless to say, fairies love the garden. Try to let part of your garden grow wild, for they far prefer this to something formal and clipped. Garden gnomes and other figures appeal to their sense of humour. A spirit may also inhabit any household item, particularly a special ornament or a teddy bear.

Once you are aware of the secret presences in your house, it will become even more of a home.

The Story of Ugunsmate

Ugunsmate is the Latvian fairy who is guardian of the hearth. There are many protective maternal spirits in Latvian rural life, and mate *is Latvian for mother. Ugunsmate is usually sensed in a strong communal feeling. When she does appear, it is often within the flames of the hearth-fire. This tale shows how Ugunsmate blessed a motherless girl, bringing her joy.*

Marta was a serving girl in a big house in Latvia, many years ago. Her parents had died when she was little, so she had no one to take care of her. Marta knew she must work hard if the family who employed her were to keep her on. However, she did not mind this. She loved fetching firewood among the trees, for she saw and spoke to the tree spirits, who were happy that she took their wood. Around the big, shadowy house Marta was very aware of other spirits, too. Some of these were not so friendly, but most were good to Marta, helping her to find lost utensils and adding traces of seasoning, to make her cooking the best in the town. Marta talked to the fairies when she was alone, but she was very careful to keep quiet if anyone else was near, lest she be called a witch. However, there was one fairy whom Marta longed to see, and never could, and this was Ugunsmate.

Ugunsmate, Marta knew, is the very spirit of the home. True, the family for whom Marta worked had little idea about the warmth of a home, for they were social climbers, very competitive and shallow. Home, to them, was a place to show off in. Actually many of their guests noticed a pleasant atmosphere, and some of them even realized this was because of the servant, Marta. The family, however, simply assumed that people came to their parties and dinners because they were so smart and entertaining.

For Marta, a feeling of homely warmth was very important. Even if the family did not appreciate what she did, she wanted to forge a link with the spirit of place. She wanted this for the animals and spirits that were in the

house, and for the little children. She also wanted it for herself, because she had no roots, no "tribe" of her own. Marta knew that Ugunsmate was a spirit that centered especially around the hearth, and every time she built up the fire she said softly, "Ugunsmate, Ugunsmate, Lady mother of the hearth, please come!" But Ugunsmate never appeared.

Marta had a single, cherished possession. This was a golden necklace with a golden locket, which she wore waking and sleeping. The chain had belonged to her mother, and Marta treasured it as her only link with her spiritual home. Often, when she was alone, she would sit musing, with her hand against her heart, holding the locket. One dreadful day Marta put her hand up to her breast, and the locket was gone! She searched high and low, even leaving several of her chores undone, but nowhere could she find it. She searched in the yard, the cowshed, the kitchen—she even groped in the flour bin and turned out the stack of firewood, all to no avail.

That night, her jobs for the day finally done, Marta sat down beside the dying embers of the fire and let her shoulders slump in despair. Her shaking hand went to her breast, feeling again the awful void where her locket should have been. Tears ran down her cheeks—it was as if she was losing her mother all over again. She stared at the fire through watery eyes, and the embers seemed to brighten. She blinked, convinced that her tears were causing her to see what was not there, but sure enough the fire was strengthening, and deep in the embers something was glowing. She tried to look closely at the fire, but the heat made her eyes water all the more. She was about to turn away, but something made her change her mind.

Marta picked up the poker, making the flames leap. She scooped at the coals and fished out—her necklace! Overjoyed, she drew it out onto the hearth to cool. "Oh, thank you, thank you!" she cried, to no one in particular. She looked into the fire, now burning strongly, and there in the flames she saw a merry woman, nodding and smiling and holding out her arms in blessing. "Ugunsmate!" breathed Marta, "Oh, thank you, with all my heart!"

WHAT THE STORY MEANS

The message is a simple one: loving and caring, tending a home and respecting a sense of "place" invites good fairies, such as Ugunsmate, to come close. These bring with them even more blessings. Look after your home, and your home will look after you.

Familiars

*We humans are not nearly as wonderful as we think, and yet there is
something special about us! We form a unique link between spirit and
matter, and our self-awareness gives us great
power, for good or ill. Some spirits think
we are worth helping, and these will
often take the form of familiars.*

In times gone by, witches were
believed to have "familiars"—that
is, an evil spirit that did the wicked will
of the witch and was usually some
sort of a link with Satan. That view is
very twisted and ignorant. No self-
respecting familiar would have
anything to do with Satan, were he to
exist; they have far better things to do.

A familiar is a guardian spirit that
helps a person through life. This may
take the form of an animal, or an
animal may have a rapport with the
spirit and behave accordingly. Animals
are a wonderful interface with the

spirit world because they are creatures
of instinct and do not judge or
condemn. Such a spirit may also take
up residence in an object, such as a
crystal, a statue, or even a teddy bear.

The term "familiar" derives from
the Latin *famulus*, which means

servant. These spirits willingly give of their strength and knowledge to humans, connecting them to the psychic realm. They are found in many cultures, from Aborigines to Zulus and from Asians to Native Americans, as well as in Europe. Familiars have various names. A "co-walker" is a fairy double, which keeps a person company; and in Icelandic culture it is considered rude to shut a door too quickly behind a person, for fear of shutting out the co-walker or "fylgia."

The familiar is generally a cozy and accessible sprite, and may act as the "genius" of the person, helping him or her to be creative, make inspired choices, and glimpse the future.

If you have a sense of being protected, that somehow things fall into place around you or that strange coincidences shape your life, suspect the presence of a familiar. If you have a much-loved and wise pet—there is your familiar! And if you would very much like one, light a candle beside a special crystal and ask for a familiar to enter it. Pledge a particular gift for animals or the environment, and the chances are that your request will be answered.

Brownies

*Brownies are lone fairies who become attached to a particular
house. They live in dark corners or cupboards within the
house, or sometimes in a hollow tree nearby. They love to
do odd jobs around the house and keep things tidy.
Brownies become affronted and may be driven
off altogether by too generous a reward, but
they do like a dish of cream to be left for them.*

The Laird of Dalswinton had a
beautiful daughter, and the
household brownie loved her dearly.
In addition to cleaning the silver and
sweeping the floors, this brownie also
advised his mistress in matters of the
heart, and helped her choose correctly
from among her many suitors. After
her wedding she soon became
pregnant—possibly helped by a little
fertility magic from the brownie! As
she went into labor, a storm raged and
the servant could not cross the river to
fetch the midwife. The stalwart

brownie changed himself into a double
of the servant, leapt astride his horse
and forded the raging river. Soon he
was back with the terrified midwife in
tow, ready to ease his mistress's birth-
pangs as soon as possible.

The brownie went into the stable
to unbridle his horse, and as he did so
he returned to his usual form, about
3 ft. (1 m) in height and clad in rags.
Unknown to him, the minister had
persuaded the laird that the brownie
should be baptized and was now
lurking in the shadows, waiting for

him. As the industrious brownie began sweeping the stable, the minister leapt toward him, flinging holy water in his face and intoning prayers.

The poor brownie gave a shriek of horror and disappeared, never to be seen again. From then on, the fortunes of the laird and his family dwindled, and though his beloved mistress still seemed to enjoy a special protection in life, the brownie was never again seen in this world.

Brownies love order, because it clears the mind and frees the heart. Far from being boring, order opens the way to magic. Part of the "order" that brownies love is their own protocol. Everything in its place: food in the cupboard, animals in the stable, and

prayers (if you must) in church. Anything out of place destroys order, overcomplicates, and confuses.

If you suspect a brownie is at work in your home—lucky you! Remember to play by *his* rules, not yours, and you will be well blessed.

Lar Familiaris

The household Lar "of the family" is the Roman version of the helpful house fairy, and some students of folklore say that beliefs about house fairies spread with the Roman Empire (house fairies themselves think this is a very funny idea, considering that they saw thousands of years come and go before the Romans were even heard of).

The Lar is one name for a protective fairy that is attached to a family and looks after its wealth and interests. Sometimes the Lar may send warning of the future in omens, and often there will be a family tradition attached to this, such as the appearance of a flock of white birds on the rooftop when someone is about to die. Such manifestations may be the work of the Lar, who might also wreak vengeance on anyone who harms a family member.

Offerings were made to the Lar at mealtimes, by pouring out a little wine on the earth and some crumbs of food. Milk was also put out as a reward, and the dregs were usually left in the milk pail for the Lar. The favorite haunt of the Lar was (and is) the hearth, because this is the heart of the home. To mark this, each month a garland of flowers or other produce would be freshly made and hung over the hearth. Full moon may have been a favored time for this, and as the moon marks female rhythms, the guiding spirit here is motherly and feminine. In addition, milk was considered a sacred gift of the Mother Goddess, so it was only fitting to return some to her, out of respect.

It is always hard to make a clear distinction between fairies and ghosts of the dead, and the likelihood is that some ghosts may take on the habits of fairies. The Lar may also be the spirit of an important ancestor, who was honored and propitiated. Sometimes people were buried under the floor of the family home, and so were believed to be still there, in residence. The Lar may be an embodiment of this spirit, or something else entirely. At all events, this strong and protective presence is to be treasured and respected.

Penates

The Penates were also house fairies and companions to the Lares
(plural of Lar). In many ways they were similar to the Lares, for their
function was also to protect and guide the family. However, although
they were associated with the hearth and the central atmosphere of the
home, in addition they were linked with the storeroom and the harvest.

The function of the Penates was to ensure that the family was always well provided with nourishment, that the harvest was successful and that all the fruit and produce were plentiful and well stored.

Images of the Penates were made in ivory, wax, or pottery and were often placed within their own shrine in the home. A light would be kept burning to honor them, and a dish of salt was placed before them. Salt was greatly valued as a preservative and as a gift of the Goddess. It is a great cleanser, both actually and metaphorically, and is credited with the ability to keep evil spirits at bay. Thus salt was an expression of the power of the Penates to preserve and guard.

Like many fairies, Penates were gods that ensured prosperity and safety, but they were demoted in status to be "just" fairies. The Penates are linked with Vesta, Roman goddess of the hearth. One way of understanding them is as the representative of Vesta within each individual home. The Romans also respected the Penates Publici, who performed

sprites were once accepted, valued, and respected companions in the home. Gradually, as the centuries passed, they became trivialized and were seen as mischievous creatures, sometimes linked with the Devil. Fairies being what they are, many have obliged and turned to pranks, to jolt complacent humans out of their beliefs that they have all the answers to the Universe and its life.

the same function in respect of the state as the household Penates did for individual families.

There is much overlap between the Lares and Penates, and they may all be understood as spirits of place, guardians of the family, and nature spirits, tending everything that grows and provides for human needs. These

As in days of yore, Lares and Penates deserve honor and respect. Evolving family traditions that do just that will enhance the atmosphere of the home and make family members feel more secure and cared for.

Hobgoblins

These are fairies of the "hob" or hearth, who are covered with hair and are good-natured—until someone offends them, when they can become troublesome. Another name for them is hobthrust, and they are really part of the brownie tribe.

Hobgoblins live in farms (especially dairies), but also love the warmth of the hearth and may come into the home, to be near one. Sometimes they can be hard to get rid of, and may become a nuisance.

One such English sprite was once attached to Sturfit Hall in Yorkshire. This hobgoblin built up the fires, churned the milk, and did many other useful things, until his mistress felt sorry for the fact that he had no clothes. She gave him a cloak and hood, whereupon he exclaimed that he would do no more good in such a garment, and vanished, never to be seen again. Another hobthrust worked for an innkeeper at Carlow Hill, and was paid for his labors with a thick piece of bread and a large pat of butter each night. One night the busy innkeeper forgot to leave out the snack, and the hobthrust was never seen again.

Hobgoblins who are insulted might turn into evil boggarts. These are covered in dark hair and have long, yellow teeth. In a bad mood they can cause havoc in a house, steal the meals of children, and even eat wood. Some may even hide in butter churns and travel with an unfortunate family to their new home. Some boggarts are believed to hide in holes in the moors, where they lie in wait for naughty children. Eventually they tire of their sport and find something better to do.

One especially nasty boggart was found in the English county of Lancashire, in the windy lanes around the town of Longridge. It was generally seen from behind at first, and looked like a little old woman in a shawl and bonnet. When the boggart turned round, however, all that appeared under the bonnet was empty space. The boggart's head was in fact in the basket she carried, and this would cackle with laughter and try to bite the poor traveler that had caught up with her.

And the moral of this story? Be kind to fairies within the home, for like all of us they can be moody, and it may take more than a box of chocolates and a bunch of flowers to win them round. The realm of the fairies is, and always will be, tricky to humans. Respect is the key.

Honoring Your Household Fairies

Honoring your household fairies will turn your house into a home, with a lovely atmosphere. It will draw luck your way and will also give your pastry a lift and your washing a gleam. Loss of the art of homemaking is responsible for many ills in our culture. One way to redress this is by respecting the spirits of place.

If you have set aside an altar space for fairies in your home, you can honor your household spirits by putting a figure of Vesta there, and a candle in a lantern. An old photo can pay homage to your ancestors. House fairies are all around your home and form part of daily life, so it is good to include them in this.

Hang a horseshoe over your door, for good luck and for the fairies to swing on! And when you pick a leaf or two from the herbs on your windowsill, say a special "Thank you" to the plant and to the fairy who helped them grow. At mealtimes say a simple grace, such as "Thanks be to the life given, to feed ours. Thanks for all that grows." Place a little food out for the fairies after meals, as described in the section on the Lar (see page 286). Use natural substances in cooking as much as possible, and avoid the microwave, for fairies do not like this.

If you have an open fire, be especially aware of its significance, not just in terms of warmth, but symbolically. Symbols of fertility, such as corn-dollies or a crystal geode, can be placed there. If you do not have an open fire, the center of your home may well be the kitchen cooker and/or the dining area. Hang a corn-dolly over your cooker and give a candle pride of place on your dining table. Light it before each meal, to make an occasion of it, and ask all good spirits to be present and give blessing.

In olden times people were aware of spirits all around them, and many things were attributed to fairies that we now look to science to explain. The world has lost its soul, leaving behind a "nothing but" attitude. Deep inside, however, most of us sense that this is far being from the true picture. In the privacy of your own home you can start to make contact with the Otherworld.

Drawing Close to Your Household Fairies

Try this spell when you want to tune into the fairies who protect and guard your home and make it the special place it is.

METHOD

1 Pick a time when you are on your own in the house, or at least sharing it only with people who are prepared to be peaceful with you. Sit comfortably in your favorite place and close your eyes. Imagine yourself leaving your body, as a spirit, and wandering around your home. Linger in each room, looking about you. Float up to the ceiling, pass through walls, into cupboards, and even below the floorboards, if that feels right.

2 What part of the house especially draws you? What areas feel welcoming and special? Do you feel compelled to do anything in a part of the home that you do not do now? Is there some artifact—a toy, a special tool, or a vase—to which you feel particularly attracted? Or anything that repels?

3 Ask the fairies in your home to show themselves to you. What happens? Do you see, hear, smell, or feel anything?

4 When you are ready, come back to everyday awareness. If you have identified somewhere special in your home, honor it with a bunch of dried herbs, a lighted candle or anything else that feels right.

Spell to Protect Your Home

This spell is no substitute for locking your doors—so be sensible and act on the material plane, too!

METHOD

You will need some salt in an earthenware pot, and some spring water in a jug.

1 Sit for a moment with the pot of salt on your lap, cradled in your palms. Ask the good house fairies to be present in whatever guise you prefer. Say something like, "Please be with me, to help protect my home." Imagine them drawing close. If you like, you can trace a five-point star with your forefinger in the salt, for this is an old symbol of the Goddess. Do the same over the spring water. Then place some salt in the water.

2 Now go round your home and sprinkle a little salt water on each doorway and window. Say something along the lines of:

Salt and water, pure and strong,
Guard my home from any wrong.

3 Imagine the house spirits coming with you, enhancing what you do with their magic. Walk round the edge of your property also, sprinkling and sealing thoroughly.

4 When you have finished, give thanks and empty the water on the ground. Keep the salt you have blessed for special dishes, or to repeat the spell.

Meditation to Draw Close to the House Fairies

This meditation will make you aware of another dimension, bringing you into contact with the spirits of place.

METHOD

1 Relax within your home and make sure that you will not be disturbed. Because you are doing this meditation in your own home, you could find it a little unnerving at first, so mentally surround yourself with an egg of light, as protection. A ring of salt, candles, daisies, or the protective herb St. John's wort will also help you feel safe. However, by doing this you may offend benevolent fairies, who cannot understand how humans can be so stupid as not to realize who is what!

2 Become very aware of your body and surroundings. How do you feel? Do you feel safe, warm, and comfortable? If not, why not? If you are uncomfortable due to material

circumstances, adjust them before proceeding. If the cause is something more subtle, try to identify what this is, as far as you are able.

3 What sounds are there in the house around you? Can you hear creaks and movements? Try to listen beyond the hum of the refrigerator and the gurgle of water in the pipes. What scents are you aware of? Is there a subtle fragrance, or any smell that reminds you of the past or of something special?

4 Imagine now that beings are coming toward you, from the corners of your house. They may be tall and stately, small and dainty, or swarthy and hairy. You may also see a deceased relative or a long-dead ancestor that you recognize by some sign. If all the

fairies seem benign, apologize to them for your protective measures.

5 Speak to these fairies. Ask them what you can do to make better contact with them. Request advice concerning your home. One of the fairies may act as a spokesperson, or you may be taken to a part of your home and shown something. If this is the case, take careful note.

6 Occasionally this exercise may reveal to you that there are presences in your home that do *not* feel good. If this is the case, say a firm "Go away" and bring yourself back to everyday awareness, immediately but gently. Consult page 38 for advice on unfriendly spirits.

7 When you have come back to everyday awareness, your home may well feel different to you, having contacted the spirits of place. Retain this awareness, and always respect the fairies. Repeat the meditation from time to time as feels right.

Flower Fairies

The Beauty of Flower Fairies

*Flowers are one of Nature's most wonderful gifts. How can
something so exquisite, so fragrant, so delicate, appearing in so many
vibrant colors and different shapes, arise out of the dusky earth?
The answer is through the work of the flower fairies.*

There are many flower fairies with a variety of tasks, and they come in a myriad of shapes and sizes. There are gnomes who work to enrich the soil, and elves whose special job it is to create brilliant and delicate colors. Other fairies cause the flower to emit its special fragrance, while still others work to ensure the health of root, stem, and leaf, so that nutrients are transferred and the propagation of the plant ensured. Certain beings take care of larger areas, such as gardens, fields, and stretches of woodland, and these are similar to the devas (see page 15). In addition, each bloom has its own special fairy that lives within it and shares its life. When the flower dies,

this fairy ceases to be and its energies become once more part of the earth, until it is time for new growth the following spring. Fairies of perennial flowers withdraw within the dormant plant, nurturing it until the time comes to grow again, while other sprites move on to different tasks in the surrounding environment.

All flowers carry a strong vibration. This applies also to cut flowers, for they continue to live if placed in water, and the fairies are still active, causing scent to be emitted and buds to open. However, the methods used to produce some flowers for sale are questionable, and while there could never be a flower that was not magical,

WARWICK GOBLE.

it is often better to have flowers growing in a pot, for they are home to more fairies, for longer. Never keep dead flowers in the house, for instead of giving you energy and inspiration, they will do the opposite. Other elemental creatures are at work, aiding the process of decay, and these may leach your own energies. Dying flowers belong on a compost heap, preparing to enrich the soil.

Flowers are so often given as gifts because they *are* gifts, from the fairies to us. Flower fairies are the gentlest, sweetest, and most generous of all sprites, and you can meet them in any garden or hedgerow.

The Lakota Tale of Prairie Rose

The following story illustrates the dedication to beauty of the flower fairies, and their love for the earth, which has given them life. There is a sense of willing sacrifice about much of the plant kingdom—shown here by Prairie Rose fairy redeeming the earth and spreading gentleness.

Long ago, in the time before time, there were no people on the earth and no animals. The prairies were covered with dull grasses and dry shrubs. Mother Earth longed to express the beauty that was within her and to wear a robe that was bright and lovely.

"The spirits of so many wonderful flowers dwell deep within me," she said to herself. "I wish they would come forth and brighten my garments. I dream of flowers white as the summer clouds and blue as the clear sky; of pink flowers, like the rosy dawn, and red flowers, glowing like the sunset; of yellow and orange flowers, like the bright midday, and purple flowers, like the velvet midnight."

A gentle pink flower heard her lament, and begged her not to worry. "I will go out onto your cloak, dear Mother," she whispered, "I will make it beautiful."

So out she went to dance upon the prairies, but the Wind Demon spotted her. "What's *her* game?" he grumbled. "I won't have her in my playground." He huffed and puffed, and roared and whistled, until she was completely flattened and her spirit returned to Mother Earth.

The flower spirits loved their mother, and one by one they offered to go out and decorate her cloak, and one by one their life was extinguished, and they fled once more to her heart.

At last Prairie Rose offered to go. "My dear child, you may take your turn," said Mother Earth. "You are so sweet and pure that even the Wind Demon will love you. I am sure he will not drive you from the plains."

So Prairie Rose began her long journey into the light, and Mother Earth prayed that this time she would succeed.

From afar the Wind Demon spotted her and began to roar. "Who dares to get in my way?" he shouted. "Why are you coming out into my playground? I will drive you away, as I did the others." He whooshed toward her, growling and roaring, but as he took his deepest breath to make his strongest gust, he smelt the sweet

fragrance of Prairie Rose, and a great calm came over him.

"Oh, what a wonderful scent!" he whispered to himself. "I cannot flatten so lovely a creature. I cannot be without her. What can I do to please her and keep her with me? I will be soft and quiet. I will caress her gently and sing to her. Then she will stay." From that day forward, Wind Demon was no longer a demon. He became a gentle spirit, singing songs of joy, and the prairie grasses danced as he passed over them. Seeing that the prairie was safe, the other flowers found their way to the surface once more, peeping through the dark earth and blossoming ever more gloriously. Now the cloak of Mother

Earth was bright with every color there is, and her heart was joyful. The Wind learnt to adore all the flowers, laughing with glee at their sweet up-turned faces and gently tweaking their petals. The bravery and beauty of Prairie Rose changed the appearance of the world for all time.

Sometimes the Wind becomes boisterous, tossing the blooms and shouting at the top of his voice. But then he remembers his darling Prairie Rose and calms down and becomes docile again. He would never, ever cause hurt to any person whose cloak is the color of Prairie Rose. He has been tamed by beauty.

WHAT THE STORY MEANS

This story shows how beauty and gentleness can be stronger than anything—even than the tempest. Prairie Rose has no power, apart from her loveliness and the sweetness of her breath, yet just by being there she transforms a demon into a being who brings music and joy to the earth. She has the courage simply to be herself. This is the very essence of the flower fairies, who daily transform our world just by their presence. They are a sign of the generosity that lies within the heart of Mother Earth, and a living proof that love conquers all.

Rose Fairy

Roses carry an especially strong vibration, and the rose fairy has a
particular power. Roses were sacred to Isis, the Egyptian goddess, said
to be the most complete goddess-form ever evolved.

Isis is mother, queen, wife, widow, lover, and mistress of magic. Resourceful and powerful, she reassembled the dismembered corpse of her husband, Osiris, after he was murdered by the envious Set. She created a new phallus by her enchantment and impregnated herself, to give birth to her son, Horus. Osiris then became Lord of the Underworld. Isis is depicted with the throne of Egypt on her head, to indicate that it is by the power of the Goddess alone that the sovereign rules the land.

The rose fairy carries with her much of the power of all the other flower fairies. Her blessings are glorious and she has links with higher beings, such as the devas. Red roses are linked with passionate love, and this languorous, warm spirit is willing to work for lovers anywhere. She also brings gifts of fertility and heady pleasure, which are in fact a sacrament. One of the messages of the red rose fairy is that sexual love is a gift of the Goddess and very sacred.

The white rose fairy awakens a more spiritual response. This is not to say that the bodily bliss of the red rose fairy is not spiritual, for the Divine resides within the material world. However, the message of the white rose fairy is to look beyond and to develop our ideas about the future.

The pink rose fairy brings affection, closeness, and gentleness. Her gift is balance, and the sort of relaxed attitude that enables us to see how we are connected to all of life.

The yellow rose fairy brings us the courage to shine forth in our own special way, to "walk our talk" and live true to our inner natures.

Any spells, or even wishes, that are about love will be given extra potency by the rose fairy, if roses are kept nearby or, even better, worn as a coronet or garland (remove all thorns first!). Rose petals scattered in the house are a calming influence, while red rose petals in bath water attract love, and roses in the garden ensure that a host of fairies will be present.

Iris Fairy

The iris fairy is very special among the inhabitants of the Land of the Fairies. Iris was the Greek goddess of the rainbow, and the rainbow is more than a glorious showing forth of all the colors of the spectrum. It is also a bridge between this world and the subtle realms, of which fairies are a part.

The "crock of gold" at the base of the rainbow is truly the realization that there are other worlds, other dimensions, and these are inhabited by magical beings—in other words, fairies. Because of this connection with the "rainbow bridge," iris fairy has the power to open your eyes to the entire fairy kingdom.

Bright with promise, iris fairies show themselves in all the hues of the rainbow. They bring cleansing, freshness, and hope for new starts in a better future. The pure vibration of these fairies clears the aura and bestows creative inspiration. Motives are pure under the influence of these beings.

The three points of the iris flower symbolize three qualities: faith, courage, and wisdom. These attributes are gifts of the iris fairy, who can truly teach you to trust in life, so that you are able to go with the flow and accept that matters will turn out well for you in the end. Iris also gives you bravery, to grapple with and change the things that really do require struggle. Last, but certainly not least, she opens your eyes to wisdom, so that you know when to act and when to wait.

Iris has been used since Roman times to purify living space and uplift the human heart. Invite the iris fairy into your life by placing fresh flowers in the area to be cleansed. All flower fairies have a special connection to the earth and to their own plant, but iris fairy can be invited into your dwelling by hanging crystals in your window, to cast tiny rainbows over the room. She will lend you her presence, bringing a breath of new life and a promise that, however dark things may seem, Truth and Beauty really do walk this earthly realm.

Lavender Fairy

The lavender flower is modest in appearance, but wonderfully fragrant. Lavender has many therapeutic and magical uses. It soothes a number of ills, from headaches to stings and rashes, and has an effect that is both cleansing and calming.

The lavender fairy is on good terms with fairies such as the household brownies, and likes to see things orderly and clean. Lavender clears blockages in the mind, and thus may enable you to think more clearly, or to release hurts. The lavender fairy also has a protective streak, and champions the cause of any woman treated cruelly by her partner. Lavender should be carried to maintain connection with the fairy and should be smelt regularly. Add lavender to your bath, and the lavender fairy will enable you to feel cleansed internally as well as externally. Place it in your drawers to encourage the lavender fairy to keep your home clean and tidy and to ensure peace prevails.

The lavender fairy can also help you to attune your psychic powers. Carrying lavender will help you to see spirits—including the lavender fairy herself! If you have a special wish, place a sprig of lavender underneath your pillow and concentrate on your wish as you fall asleep. If it is destined to come true, you will dream about your wish. However, if you do not dream, or simply dream about something else, then your wish will not be fulfilled. Try not to let this bother you. The lavender fairy can bring you something much better. Close your eyes and be calm, while you inhale the lavender fragrance, and you will find that all sorts of other solutions come to mind.

Perhaps the greatest gift of the lavender fairy is happiness. Look at the plant if you feel down, stroke its fragrant spikes and inhale its scent. Burn lavender oil in an oil burner or diffuser, to lighten your heart and clear your mind. Those who smile all the time are said to be the longest-lived, and yet another gift of lavender fairy is longevity.

Buttercup Fairy

Sunny buttercup fairy brings you awareness of your gifts and helps you to feel confident, able to explore and express your talents in this lifetime. The golden "cup" of this flower is full of bounty and cheer. The buttercup fairy is compassionate and has a deep understanding of human beings.

Her healing energies are abundant, and if you have been feeling worthless and dejected, this fairy will help, enabling you to spot new opportunities and think positive, for after all life is full of sunshine and new chances.

There is a little custom in the West Country of England of picking a buttercup and holding the up-turned "cup" underneath the chin of a child (or responsive adult!) and saying, "Do you like butter?" If the golden color reflects off the person's chin, then yes, they *do* like butter. Of course, every chin glows yellow! Whether you really like butter or not, this playful action is very cheering, for it brings the buttercup fairy close to the throat chakra, which is the spiritual center that rules communication.

The touch of the buttercup fairy makes you feel special.

Clover Fairy

Clover has a leaf with three lobes, sometimes linked with the Triple Goddess: Maiden, Mother, and Crone. The three-leafed clover can be carried as a protective charm. To find a four-leafed clover is, however, extremely lucky. Such leaves are rare, and may be taken to symbolize the four Elements of Earth, Fire, Air, and Water, which is very magical.

Clover itself is an enchanted plant, often growing close to where Leprechauns are sighted. Clover fairies are dainty and graceful. They love people who show respect for the natural world and bring gifts of true love and loyalty to those who genuinely seek them.

Clover fairies may be spotted as tiny lights, fluttering around the flower—look beyond the flower, not at it, in order to glimpse them. White clover fairies respond most to the full moon. Clover can help you to open your psychic sight. Ask the fairy if you may help yourself to her gifts and, if the answer is "yes," pull out the petals of clover and suck the honey within. Then you will be able to see spirits— starting with the clover fairy herself.

Daisy Fairy

*Daisies often grow on lawns and readily spring back up after the grass
has been cut. The daisy fairy is very robust and does not worry about
humans and their actions. For this reason she can be an effective guide
into the realms of fairyland. Many other fairies are drawn close to
daisies. A special gift of the daisy fairy is resilience and creativity.*

A wonderful way to make contact
with nature spirits of all kinds is
to sit in a meadow and make a daisy
chain. Do this lazily and quietly, letting
yourself drift and dream. Wear the
daisy chain when you are meditating—
for instance, doing the exercises at the
end of this section (see pages 332–335).
This will invite the fairies close.

The daisy fairy also draws love.
Carry a daisy to do this, and if your
lover has left you, folk wisdom advises
you to sleep with a daisy-root beneath
your pillow. In this way the tenacity of
the flower will transfer itself to your
relationship, and you will be reunited
with your love.

Gorse Fairy

Gorse flowers all the year round and it is one of the functions of the gorse fairy to be cheering, even when the situation seems hopeless. She averts despair and shows a light at the end of any tunnel.

The gorse fairy is also very protective, repelling evil of both a physical and spiritual nature. Fairies of all descriptions are said to cluster in gorse bushes, especially on May Eve. The gorse fairy is also helpful in attracting money.

There is an old saying: "Whenever the gorse is in flower, kissing's in season." So love is in season all year round. The gorse fairy is associated with passion, fertility, and creativity. Gorse is sacred to the Celtic god of light, Lugh, who is a god of many talents. He brings inspiration and craftsmanship. Gorse fairy sets the hills aflame, and the heart aflame likewise. Gorse's golden flowers link it with the sun, and its evergreen leaves speak of the life that is ever-present in the cycle of the seasons. Gorse is a feisty, powerful fairy. She bids you listen to your creative hunches and follow the whims of your imagination.

Honeysuckle Fairy

Scent is the most primitive of the senses, connecting to the reptilian brain stem. Fragrance has great power to evoke old memories and buried feelings, and this is well understood by the honeysuckle fairy.

She can bring the past into the present, or enable you to let go of old habits that may have become destructive. She can also heighten your psychic powers. Ask her if you may crush her blooms and hold them on your forehead, to open your third eye.

Honeysuckle fairy brings secret gifts that can lend you an air of mystery and sensuality, so that others are drawn to you. She also brings luck, especially when honeysuckle grows near your house. However, there are more profound gifts associated with honeysuckle fairy, for she offers initiation into the mysteries of Nature. Like all true mysteries, this is an open mystery— there to be seen by all who have eyes to see. Honeysuckle's wisdom is that the Divine resides within the sensuous: a simple idea, but hard to perceive. Let honeysuckle show you the way, and enjoy every minute!

Bluebell Fairy

Bluebells carpet the woodland in late spring, creating a shimmering azure haze in which thousands of fairies dance. This is similar to the hue of the human "etheric," which is the part of the aura closest to the body and easiest to see.

Bluebell fairies have an affinity with this energy, stimulating the life force of the earth as the summer is ushered in. These are magical flowers, and to have them in your garden used to be considered proof of being a witch. They are also reputed to grow where Oakmen fairies dwell (see page 348).

Bluebell fairies bring special enchantment, opening the doors to the fairy realm so that all may get a glimpse through them. Enchantment is not about losing your grip on reality, but about literally being "en-chant-ed"— that is, "within a song." This is to see life as it truly is: a wonderful vibration where beauty and emotion, the internal and external, are one. The bluebell is shaped like a bell, and bluebell fairy brings "the ring of truth." It is said that anyone who carries a bluebell cannot tell a lie. In fact, such a person must be true to himself or herself, for that is the most important truth of all.

Primrose Fairy

The primrose forms a special portal to the fairy realms, and a primrose-studded bank around the time of the Spring Equinox is a very good place to see fairies of all kinds. Blue and red primroses growing in the garden attract fairies, too, and keep the household from harm.

The primrose fairy is innocent, delicate, and fresh. She brings clear perspectives on life and a feeling of renewal. For this reason, primroses were believed to cure madness. Look into the sweet face of the primrose and everything in the Universe will appear to be in its right place. The purity of the primrose fairy also brings loyalty and love. Primroses were sewn into the pillowcases of children to ensure they would be affectionate and loyal. Like so many fairies, primrose fairy attracts love, especially towards women who wear her flower.

Primrose fairy can make the invisible worlds visible, for she shows all, in truth and purity. Eating primroses is believed to enable you to see fairies. To knock on a fairy rock with a posy of primroses is to open the door to Fairyland, but it is important to have the right number of blooms in the bouquet for the magic to work.

Cowslip Fairy

The cowslip is a variety of primrose, appearing a little later in the spring, and a potent indication of fairy activity. Like the primrose fairy, the cowslip fairy has a youthful innocence, and she will help to keep young anyone who carries her bloom.

I f you are feeling old and jaded, and that the best years have passed you by, she will restore your zest for life and your belief that anything can happen. She can also make you look younger, partly because youthfulness is a light in the eye and a spring in the step, and the cowslip fairy can give you these.

Cowslips have a sweet and magical scent that is quite subtle, breathing the very essence of the earth and of spring. This scent is healing to all ills, especially those brought on by fatigue and discouragement. The cowslip fairy also knows the secrets of hidden treasure. Fairy lore states that if you carry a bunch of cowslips, the fairies will help you find hidden gold.

The cowslip fairy will also guard your privacy. Place one of her flowers beneath your doormat if you don't want anyone to come calling and you'll be left alone.

Lily Fairy

The lily fairy brings great purity and spirituality. She has links with the angels, who are cosmic messengers. In particular she is associated with the Archangel Gabriel, who is often depicted holding a lily.

Gabriel is the angel of the moon, and has links with many moon-associated gifts. These include psychic ability, for the full moon stimulates the intuition. It also brings fertility, because of its association with the female cycle and the waxing moon with pregnancy. All these are gifts of the lily fairy.

The lily fairy whispers of dreams and all the special things we need to know, deep in our hearts. The heady fragrance of the lily is erotic—lily reminds us, as so many flowers do, that physical love is innocent and pure, and that it is only we who contaminate and complicate it. Lily is most strongly connected to the winter solstice, when some traditions say the sun god is reborn, and so the lily fairy presides over the emergence of new life. Ask the lily fairy to connect you to the mysteries of rebirth and to enable you to understand the cycle of life.

Heather Fairy

The heather fairy is said to supply her bloom so that the other fairies may feed on it. The fairies do not literally feed on the plant, of course, but they may well absorb its essence, which is vibrant and protective.

This plant has been used to call up spirits, because the heather fairy has such an affinity with all other sprites and dwellers in the hidden realms. Heather is also considered very lucky. Gypsies bind it into nosegays and sell it for this reason. White heather is believed to be the luckiest of all.

The heather fairy is very protective, and carrying her flower enables you to keep all forms of violence at bay. Withdrawn and quiet people are a magnet to this fairy, and she will encourage them to express themselves in a way that is appropriate to their inner natures. With the help of the heather fairy, you may find abilities that you never dreamt you possessed! Ask if you may take from the bush, and bind a little bunch with blue twine. Place this in your buttonhole, and heather fairy will prompt you to be more outgoing.

Lilac Fairy

The nostalgic scent of lilac recalls the past and brings back long-forgotten emotions. Some of these emotions may be associated with past lives. The lilac fairy can awaken distant memories and enable you to realize that you have lived before, loved before, and understood before.

The lilac is really a tree, but the blooms are very floral and involve a great deal of fairy activity. The lilac fairy has some similarities to the bluebell fairy in that she is linked with subtle vibrations that may be understood as musical. Harmony is the great gift of the lilac fairy.

Although lilac draws many sprites, the power of its presence will also repel any that are not well-meaning. Place lilac flowers in your home if you believe it to be haunted, and the fresh blooms will drive away ghosts. Lilac also protects against evil when planted close to a property or strewn on the floor. Because lilac is a tree, the influence of the lilac fairy is enduring.

Marigold Fairy

The marigold fairy is strengthening and heartening. This is a fairy with powerful healing gifts, bringing with her the warmth of the sun to renew life and restore vigor. Folklore tells that marigolds picked at noon have the greatest power to comfort the heart, because at that time the marigold fairy will be able to reflect the potency of the sun.

The marigold fairy can also help you win admiration and respect. Ask if you may pick some of her flowers, and add these to your bath water—the radiance of the sun will attach itself to you. However, be sure the marigold is *Calendula officinalis*, and not the African marigold *Tagetes*, which is often sold as a bedding plant, but is very poisonous.

If you look at the shining flowers of marigold, your sight will be strengthened; you hearing may also benefit. Touching the flower with your bare feet may enable you to understand the language of birds, and marigold fairy brings the gift of clairaudience— that is, the ability to hear spirits and fairies. Marigolds placed beneath the bed enable the marigold fairy to stimulate prophetic dreams. Carry a marigold and the fairy will help you to obtain just treatment.

Poppy Fairy

The poppy fairy is the great bringer of dreams and visions, but to use these properly requires discrimination—they can bring confusion and even madness, or they can be correctly interpreted as offering different perspectives on life. Not all these perspectives may be available in the mortal state, but they can provide inspiration and creativity.

The poppy fairy can aid sleep. Because imagination is so closely linked to fertility of the mind, it is no surprise to learn that the poppy fairy is also associated with fertility of the body. Poppy flowers and seeds can be eaten to promote this, and to attract wealth.

The poppy fairy is most active in summer at Lammas (see page 70), when the wheat is due to be harvested and the blood-red poppies stain the golden corn. The poppy fairy has the sombre message that life must be sacrificed to enable other life to flourish. She also speaks of the life-beyond-life that always continues, endlessly reborn in the eternal cycle.

Ephemeral and yet vivid, poppy also tells us to live in the moment—for it is all there is, and it is sweet.

Snapdragon Fairy

The snapdragon is a fiery fairy who can help you repel all negative energies. Wear a snapdragon on your body and no one will ever be able to pull the wool over your eyes, for the snapdragon fairy is far too cute, and will burn away the dross, to reveal the truth.

I f you feel you have been subjected to negative influences, pick some snapdragons and place them in a vase.

Put a mirror behind them and ask the snapdragon fairy to reflect any ill-wishing back at the person from whom it came.

The snapdragon fairy has links with the fire fairies and with dragons. When picked, the snapdragon flower can be squeezed at the base, to open like a dragon's mouth; to do this respectfully and with awareness is to invoke the energies of the dragon spirits that guard these flowers. These beings can help you gain great strength and personal power, enabling you to express yourself with conviction and authority. Just as you are listening to your own inner voice, the snapdragon fairy can help you hear those of the spirit realm.

Daffodil Fairy

The daffodil fairy blows the trumpet that ushers in the spring. As the fresh winds toss the daffodil flower, so the fairy within brings a message of clarity and new beginnings. The daffodil fairy can help you not only understand your true potential, but also tell the world about it. To the daffodil fairy we are all beautiful, and she helps us to see ourselves in this way.

The daffodil is of the same family as the narcissus, and the original Narcissus was a handsome youth, who was loved by a nymph called Echo. But Narcissus was too self-absorbed to notice Echo and sat all day by the water's edge, admiring his own reflection. Poor Echo faded away, until all she could do was repeat what other people said, while the gods turned Narcissus into a flower.

This story warns us that we can give away our power by loving in the wrong way, and that we lose our humanity—as Narcissus did—when we love only ourselves. The daffodil fairy encourages us to meditate on love.

Tulip Fairy

Like so many fairies, the tulip fairy is associated with love. The tulip is shaped like a chalice, and this is the "loving cup" from which tulip fairy encourages you to imbibe, to feel the blessings of Nature. One of the messages of the tulip fairy is to have the courage to be vulnerable, because only in this way can any of us ever know closeness and fulfillment.

The word "tulip" comes from the Turkish word for turban, which the flower shape was thought to resemble, and one of the gifts of the tulip fairy is the ability to clear the head and enable you to sort out priorities. She can help you to see what things really mean, what matters, and which people in your life are truly important to you. Tulips were sometimes worn in the turban for protection.

The tulip fairy can guard against all bad luck, while the good luck she brings comes from clarity of vision. This enables you to choose well and to distinguish the beneficial from the harmful. Place tulips on your dressing table or anywhere significant in your home, to attract love, protection, and good fortune.

Violet Fairy

The modest spirit of violet epitomizes all the qualities that are needed to attract fairies, such as humility and simplicity. In ancient Greece violets were worn to promote tranquillity and facilitate sleep.

The violet fairy (like so many of the good flower fairies) offers protection against mischievous spirits and is very lucky. When examined closely, the unobtrusive violet is exquisitely beautiful, and the violet fairy is allied to the goddess Venus. Because of this she can be very erotic, and when mixed with lavender in sachets she stimulates love and lust. She is also powerfully lucky, and it is said that if you gather the first violet of spring, your dearest wish will be granted, for all the fairies will come to your aid.

Due to her links with Venus, the violet fairy is a close ally of the Fairy Queen. Relationships are generally the province of the Feminine, and the violet fairy can help you understand where you fit in, in groups, and to become better adjusted. She also increases your psychic powers and will clear your head physically, for a chaplet of violets is said to cure headaches.

Meeting the Flower Fairies

The flower fairies are among the easiest fairies to meet, and if you love flowers, you are sure to find a connection with these beings. Every time you feel that thrill of delight or sensation of peace when you are tending growing things, you are coming under their influence.

Doing the garden is one obvious method. Try to do this in a relaxed way, delighting in the feel of the earth and trying not to be too fixated on results. The flower fairies will be close by, to help you. Although the colors of cultivated flowers may be dazzling, often the most potent sprites are to be found in wild flowers, for these carry the essence of the earth and the mystery of countless seasons of growth and decay.

Focus on a specific plant and notice every detail: the delicate shape of the flower, the variations in color, and texture. How do you feel deep inside? Your feelings are the flower fairy's way of communicating with you.

Connecting with the Flower Fairies

Concentrate on one special flower, in order to invite the fairy of that flower into your life. Surround yourself with the flower, if possible, either as pot plants or in your garden. Have pictures of the flower on your walls, and bring its color into your life as much as you can, by wearing it and by using it in your house decor, in throws, cushions, and rugs.

Research the lore of the flower and any myths associated with it. Which gods and goddesses have links with it? If you have a devotional altar, as described in previous sections of this book, place the flower there.

Many flower essences are available as essential oils, and you could either wear your chosen oil as a perfume or vaporize it in an oil burner, to attract the flower fairy. Carry the flower with you, either in its live form or as an amulet—maybe a brooch or badge. Collect symbols of associated deities. Play music of any sort that feels appropriate, and tell yourself that you are going to dream about your flower fairy when you go to bed. She will come to you and bless you.

Flower-Fairy Spells

*Each flower is a "spell" in itself, for it comes with a special quality
and power. Study the meanings of each flower, to decide what you
would like to draw into your life. Place your chosen flowers around
a candle of the same color, to intensify their influence.*

For instance, to draw love to you, light a deep-rose candle and ring it with fresh roses. Place a piece of rose quartz within the ring, and imagine the love you want coming to you. Carry the rose quartz when you go out, to attract a lover. For clarity of mind a white candle is best, ringed with clover. And to draw money your way, twine honeysuckle around a green candle and think of all the riches that are coming to you, and what you will do with them. Remember to return some of your bounty to the earth.

When flowers are pressed and dried, they retain some of their magical essence and can be used to keep the flower fairy close, or to help you attune you to that flower. Place the flower between two sheets of tissue paper on a firm surface, then cover it with a weight. After a few days the flower will be dry and ready for use.

Meditation to Meet the Flower Fairies

Do this meditation outside on a still day, close to the flower with which you wish to connect. Alternatively, perform it indoors with a pot plant or pressed flower. If you can imagine your flower very clearly, the power of your mind alone may take you to the flower-fairy realms.

METHOD

1 Relax completely, as described in the Introduction (see pages 34–35), and concentrate on your flower.

2 It seems to be getting larger and larger—or are you getting smaller? Your surroundings are becoming misty, and the mist seems to envelop you. You are conscious of the flower's wonderful fragrance seeping into you. All is indistinct, as if you are slightly intoxicated.

3 The mist gradually clears and you see that the scene around you has changed. You are now in a garden surrounded by a thick green hedge. You see paths leading from the garden: one leads down to a river winding through green fields; another to shady woodland and a cascade of bird song; yet another to a castle on the hill, with flags waving from its turrets. You realize that you are in a fairy world, where time has no meaning.

4 The garden is full of flowers of all descriptions and colors, but above all there is a profusion of your chosen flower. It is bright, vibrant, flourishing; all the blooms are perfect. As you contemplate it, you hear the sound of silvery laughter in the air.

5 From behind the hedge comes a being. This is the fairy of the flower, clad in robes the color of the flower itself, and she is the most exquisite creature you have ever seen. Laughing, she beckons to you. You follow her, brushing past flowers and stooping under tree branches. She takes you to a part of the garden where her flower grows especially thick. She picks flower after flower, and each time another immediately takes its place. She fashions the blooms into a garland for you; then she fashions a chaplet; more

flowers are cast beneath your feet. Their fragrance surrounds you, and wonderful music seems to be coming from the blooms themselves.

6 The flower fairy invites you to dance, and you do so, feeling as graceful as your magical companion. The flowers have released you from the confines of your humanity and you are part of earth and sky, as she is. You dance, sing, if you wish, and converse with the flower fairy. Do not be surprised if you feel like laughing in joy.

7 The time comes to leave the flower fairy. Thank her for her companionship and return to that part of the garden where you first found yourself. The colored mist surrounds you again, and as it slowly clears you find yourself back in the everyday world.

Meditation for the Gift of the Flower Fairy

Perform this meditation to receive a gift from the flower fairy. Treasure this, even if you are not sure what it means. In time this will become clear.

METHOD

1 Begin this meditation in the same way as before (see page 332). Allow the enchanting mist to arise around you and find yourself once more in the magical garden.

2 The fairy appears and leads you to where the flowers grow lush and wonderful. She garlands and crowns you, but this time is more solemn. Then she leads you into overgrown parts of the garden, and you find yourself at the edge of a pool.

3 You kneel and smile to see your reflection, covered in flowers. The fairy kneels beside you and, taking one of the blooms, stirs the surface of the

water with it. As she does so the scene changes. Now you see images of the world from which you have come: tracts of land too barren to support life of any kind; soil poisoned with pesticides; and countless beautiful flowers, in fields, parklands, and gardens, flourishing and blessing each person that passes—but most people simply walk by, taking no notice. They have frowns on their faces and are totally immersed in their thoughts. One person hurries to see his bank manager, his head full of figures; another clutches his phone, planning what lies to tell his wife so that he can be with his mistress; yet another is thinking about a forthcoming job interview. You realize how unimportant their concerns are— how, in a year or two, their troubles will mean nothing. Truly they could have spared themselves the grief and stopped for a few moments, for what did any of it matter beside the sheer beauty of the flowers? You make a mental note to enjoy the ordinary miracles of life around you. The flower fairy nods and smiles—she knows what is going through your mind.

4 She takes a bloom, touches the water and the scene clears, so that again you see your reflection. She turns to where a clump of flowers grows and passes her hand over one of them. This flower grows and grows until it is as large as your head. You marvel at its lushness. You realize that this pretty plant actually carries a savage power— the power of Mother Earth.

5 The flower fairy reaches into the flower and draws forth a gift for you. It may be an artifact or a written message, or you may feel a sensation or hear a tune or voice. Thank the fairy and take your leave. Return to your original place in the garden. Let yourself come back to the everyday world slowly, and treasure your gift, whatever it may be.

Tree
Fairies

The Magic of Trees

Many poems have been written about the beauty and wonder of trees. They inspire creativity and evoke a sense of peace and awe. The mysteries of life and death are embodied by trees, which have always been vital to our survival.

Besides being the lungs of the planet, breathing oxygen to enrich the air, trees give wood for houses, boats, furniture, and fires. They provide habitats for myriad creatures, both seen and unseen, and yield many medicines.

With their roots in the earth, their trunks above and their branches reaching to the skies, trees are powerfully symbolic. In ancient times, magical priests called shamans traveled in the spirit world to gain information and to fight battles for their tribe, and the tree formed a "map" of the subtle worlds. The roots are in the Underworld of ancestral spirits, the trunk is in Middleworld (which is close to this world, but includes spirits and fairies, and exists in a varied time frame) and the branches are in Upperworld, which is the realm of the gods and angels. The Norse World Tree, Yggdrasil, on which Odin hung to gain knowledge of the runes, is the most powerful example of a World Tree. However, trees have formed the background to inspiration and transformation of many kinds: in Paradise it was a tree that held knowledge of good and evil; Buddha sat beneath a tree to receive enlightenment; and the apple that revealed gravity to Newton fell from a tree!

The Native Americans call trees "The Standing People" in awareness of the fact that they are not just mindless stalks, growing out of the earth. Trees are deeply wise and individual beings. Each tree forms a portal to the Otherworld, and offers a home to many fairies, in addition to the special spirit of the tree, which is called a dryad. Trees love children, and children are in turn drawn to trees, playing beneath them and climbing them. Every child's dream is to have a tree-house in which to hide. The playfulness of children is a magnet

to fairies, for their energies are light, pure, and scintillating, and trees form a wonderful shelter and focus for this interface between the worlds.

The easiest way to approach the Otherworld is to get close to a tree. Do it whenever you can and you will find that your intuition is subtly enhanced and that you become aware of other levels of reality.

The Lady in White

Here is a tale of that most feminine of tree fairies, the Birch Lady.
She embodies the virtues of beauty, grace and the domestic arts, but
also teaches of the freedom of women to be creative and spontaneous.
For those who are inspired to break the mould, her rewards may be
generous and magical, as this story shows.

Long ago, in old Czechoslovakia, dwelt a young maiden called Bethushka. From the time when the rivers swelled with the melting snows until the leaves turned to amber, she would take her flock of sheep to graze close to the birch trees. She brought her spindle with her to spin flax, but could not resist wandering among the trees. How graceful they were, and how sweetly the wind whispered in their leaves! Often she would dance, swaying from tree to tree and humming softly as she went.

One day as she danced, she realized she was not alone in the birch grove.

There in front of her was a beautiful lady dressed in white lace and satin, with long platinum hair cascading down her back. Her eyes were a deep green and she wore a chaplet of flowers. She was smiling at Bethushka. "I can see you love dancing!" she said, and her voice was soft as the wind in the trees.

"Yes, I do love it so," said Bethushka. Somehow she felt no shame at her antics. "But really I should not be dancing—I should be spinning."

"Plenty of time for that," said the lady. "Dance with me, my child, and I will teach you new steps."

Bethushka needed no persuasion. She whirled and pirouetted with the lady, round and round the trees and out into the open fields. As they danced, they left not a footstep on the tender grass. They sang and laughed as they skipped and swayed. It seemed only a few moments until the shadows began to lengthen and the sun to go down. Bethushka scanned the sky anxiously, and when she looked back down the lady had vanished.

Sadly Bethushka shook her head. "I cannot dance with you," she said.

"I promised my mother I would spin the flax, and if I do not she will be angry with me. We are poor and she needs the money from my spinning." The white lady still held out her hand. "If you dance with me," she said, "I will make sure it is done."

This was all the encouragement Bethushka needed. She dropped her spool, took the lady's hand and whirled off into the trees again. As the sun was setting, the lady led Bethushka back to her spindle and waved her arms toward it—the spool was miraculously full of fine white thread. Bethushka ran to pick it up and, marveling, turned back to the lady, but she was gone. Tired but happy, she drove her sheep home and gave the full spool to her mother, who was delighted.

She rounded up her sheep and wended her way homeward. Her mother asked her how she had got on with her spinning, and Bethushka had to admit she had lost the spool. Her mother scolded her, and Bethushka promised to look for it the next day. She kept quiet about the lady in white and her dancing.

Morning came round and Bethushka took her sheep to the field near the birch grove once more. She found her spindle, but just as she started to get into a rhythm, the lady in white appeared. "Come, let us dance again," she said, holding out a pale, slender hand toward Bethushka.

Bethushka woke early the next day and drove her sheep eagerly to the birch grove. Again the lady in white appeared and they danced as never before. Their steps were as the breeze that lightly stirs the grass, or as the waves that curve upon the shore. When evening arrived, with a motion of her ivory hand the lady filled the spool once more. Bethushka tried to thank her, but she laughed and told her the pleasure was all hers. "You are a skillful dancer, my dear, and I have had a wonderful time with you!"

She handed Bethushka a pouch embroidered with runic symbols that Bethushka did not understand. "Look after this," said the lady as she left. Bethushka peeped inside the pouch and found it was full of dried birch leaves, but took it carefully home.

When her mother saw the second perfect spool she became suspicious. "Surely you did not do all this yourself," she said to Bethushka. Then the whole story of the lady in white and the dancing came spilling out, and her mother said, "Why, that must have been the Wild Lady of the Birch Grove! She brings great good luck to all who catch sight of her."

"It was wonderful dancing with her," said Bethushka, "and she even gave me a gift." She picked up the embroidered pouch and opened it to show her mother the leaves, but when she emptied it out they both gasped in wonderment and joy—for all the birch leaves were made of solid gold that glistened and gleamed.

WHAT THE STORY MEANS

The message of the Wild Lady of the Birch Grove is simple, but profound. Seize the day, and follow where your heart leads. Do not always hedge yourself around with "shoulds" and "oughts"—instead, be open to opportunities for enjoyment and self-expression. Perform the dance of life with joy, and if you follow the path that is right for you, your world will be full of riches.

Willow Fairy

The willow fairy can be grumpy and tricky. The Hobbits in The Lord of the Rings *were lulled to sleep and almost killed by Old Man Willow, and while fairies are rarely so ill-intentioned, the willow fairy is not always kindly.*

The willow fairy may leave the tree at night and follow travelers, muttering and mumbling, which can be rather frightening to those who do not understand.

Willow has profound wisdom to offer, which humans rarely appreciate. It is deeply mystical and in tune with the music of the waters, all around the globe. Salicylic acid, which is used to make aspirin, comes from the willow, and the willow elves are associated with knowledge of medicinal herbs and healing.

Approached with respect, willow is a wonderful teacher and will whisper to us if we listen. It is important to be still, and to understand that human perceptions are shallow. Imagine the questing roots of willow, seeking the underground streams that flow to and from the earth-girdling oceans. Nighttime is best to commune with this spirit in meaningful dreams.

Rowan Fairy

The rowan fairy is strong and protective, yet feminine and very magical. Norse myth tells that the first woman was formed from a rowan, while the ash formed the first man. Rowan is reported to have saved the life of the god Thor by bending over a swift river where he was drowning and enabling him to pull himself out.

The Druids used incense made from rowan wood to conjure spirits, yet the rowan fairy has such a grounding influence that she can connect you with the Otherworld while keeping you firmly in this world. Rowan protects against superstition and fosters a positive attitude. The rowan is planted near homes, for protection and insight.

The rowan fairy is one of the most helpful of all, for she values the matters of this world and seeks to establish a connection with the subtle realms. She repels intruders firmly, yet invites interchange between the realms of being. Rowan is very powerful near stone circles and barrow-mounds, for her abilities are enhanced in these places. Her power will come with you if you carry rowan berries in your pocket, to where the water meets the land—and this can inspire you to write poetry.

Apple Fairy

The apple fairy is extremely beautiful and frequently seductive. Apples were considered the fruit of the gods in Celtic lore, and the apple tree has many associations with magical creatures. The unicorn lives underneath it, and in spring the sweet apple blossom offers home to many flower fairies who spread an atmosphere of love and happiness.

The gifts of the apple fairy are everlasting youth and beauty, although sadly such matters often give rise to strife. For instance, the Trojan wars were caused by a competition among the Olympian goddesses about a golden apple, which was to be awarded to the fairest. Paris, prince of Troy, was called to judge, and Aphrodite promised him the most beautiful woman in the world as his wife, if he would choose her. He did so, and was awarded Helen—the only drawback being that she was already married to Menelaus. And so began the long siege of Troy.

The apple fairy invites us to enjoy sensuous pleasures of all descriptions, in the knowledge that there is plenty to go around, and that nothing that is truly ours can ever be taken away from us. It is our fault if we forget this.

Hawthorn Fairy

Along with oak and ash, hawthorn forms the "fairy triad" that is especially inviting to fairies. Hawthorn is, in some ways, the fairy tree, forming a portal to the fairy realms and holding strong magic.

The hawthorn fairy offers access to the Otherworld, but also protects the unwary, so it is important to be patient with this spirit. She can enchant your life, bringing growth and fertility to all areas, and when the hawthorn flowers in spring, it represents the bridal gown of the young Goddess.

Hawthorn is sacred to the Welsh sun goddess Olwen, the "white lady of the day." Where she trod she left white footprints of hawthorn, and her father, Yspaddaden Pencawr, was "Giant Hawthorn." Thirteen tasks were demanded of her suitor, Culhwych, before he could marry her and overcome the power of the giant.

Thirteen is a number associated with the moon, for the moon makes 13 circuits of the zodiac to one of the sun. Thus the hawthorn suggests union: of sun and moon, male and female.

The hawthorn fairy promises cleansing, fulfillment, guardianship, and fertility. Keeping grounded and practical is the best way to access her and to use her gifts.

Oak Fairy

Oak is one of the most sacred trees, traditionally prized by the Celts and Druids. The oak fairy is very powerful, and imparts strength and endurance to any who stay within its aura.

Each oak tree is a very metropolis of fairies, and each acorn has its own sprite. Bringing one into the house is a way to enhance contact with the fairy realm. Oak beams are often used to make doors, but the tree itself is a great portal to the other realms.

The oak is associated with many gods all over the world, notably Zeus and Thor. In sacred groves of oak, the Goddess was believed to impart her wisdom through oracles. The oak has sheltered many a king and hero, in myth and real life—for instance, Charles II and Robin Hood—and is associated with Herne the Hunter, or Cernunnos (see page 256). The oak spirit is distinct from fairies called Oakmen who inhabit oak copses, and may become very angry if trees are felled or wildlife harmed.

The oak fairy brings courage and a stout heart, necessary to face the challenges in this world and to journey in the Otherworld. Bearing strength from the heart of the earth, oak fairy can bring steadiness and a deep joy that endures through all.

Mistletoe Fairy

Mistletoe grows most easily on the apple tree, but is (and was) prized by the Druids especially when it grew on the oak. The mistle berries were seen as the semen of the god, come to fertilize the earth, and so a sacred marriage was believed to take place.

The mistletoe is harvested with a golden sickle, its shape paying homage to the moon, while its metal salutes the sun. Because it grows and yet does not touch the ground, mistletoe is seen as signifying the moment of incarnation, of entry-into-time, and is highly valued as a source of wisdom, the "fertility of the mind."

Despite its masculine connotations, the mistletoe fairy is rather feminine. It is also a great protector of children, as a manifestation of fertility and a promise of the future (and because fairies *love* the playfulness of a child!). These fairies are very wise, and can convey knowledge of how to remain invisible, and how to blend into the background and so observe all the more acutely. Mistletoe and oak together bring images of the future and knowledge of the soul's true home and purpose.

Hazel Fairy

Hazel is a mercurial sprite, deeply wise—a bringer of insight and flashes of inspiration. This fairy can help you to find knowledge in a very individual way, and to develop your intuition, so that you can see deeply into many things.

Hazel holds the secrets of the earth, and can teach about dowsing and the currents within the land, known as ley lines. She also encourages meditation and confers eloquence on those who respect and honor her.

Druids carry hazel staffs, to enhance knowledge and to use as "talking sticks." Irish lore tells of how the salmon of wisdom swam in Connla's well, eating the hazelnuts that fell from the nine hazel trees surrounding it. And legend describes how the trickster hero, Fion mac Cumhail, came to the well to learn

wisdom from the poet Finegas; he obtained insight illicitly, by roasting a salmon and sucking a drop of its juice that landed on his thumb.

The story of Fion indicates that inspiration and insight may be acquired by devious means. The hazel fairy understands this, but there is one type of deviousness that is resourceful, and another that is closer to deceit. Fairies appreciate the former, while the latter gets short shrift!

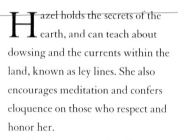

Holly Fairy

Traditionally, the holly is king of the waning year, from midsummer to midwinter, and the oak is king of the waxing year, from midwinter to midsummer. These "kings" may be seen as different aspects of the God, battling for the hand of the Goddess, who is the earth herself.

Holly is another tree sacred to the Druids, who brought it within their homes in winter to offer shelter to the fairies. Like the oak, holly provides a home to many sprites, and its spirit is a guardian and a warrior. The holly fairy brings courage and the warrior spirit. He will help you with any internal or spiritual struggles, and can awaken powerful healing abilities.

Holly is especially sacred at the Winter Solstice, serving to usher in the new life of the sun god. Its evergreen leaves are a sign of endurance. If you meditate close to a holly bush you may receive warning or encouragement from the holly fairy.

Elder Fairy

The elder is a tree of beginnings and endings, of birth and death,
so the elder fairy is a spirit of transformation and the crossing of
thresholds. Generally seen as an old woman, the elder fairy advises
on what to cast away and what to take up.

S he may provide a potent link with the Mother Goddess and facilitates contact with spirits of other trees. In a sense she acts as a mother figure within the woodland. She carries the wisdom of the Crone, and is mistress of the deepest magic.

Elder has many associations with witches and pagans: witches were said to be able to turn themselves into elder trees. Gypsies believe that it is very bad luck to cut down and burn elder wood and that the Elder Mother will take revenge. This superstition arises from an instinctive realization that a lack of respect for Nature is dangerous, ultimately, to the human race. Elder's unruly growth hints at the untameable aspect of Nature, the black heart of the earth to which we owe our being.

Elder fairy has an aged, feminine wisdom, too long misprized in our culture, but with a little respect she will act as teacher.

Ash Fairy

The ash fairy is androgynous and ambiguous, carrying great mysticism and power and making many connections: between this world and the Otherworld, between masculine and feminine, and between differing ideas. The ash fairy understands that problems are rarely solved on the level at which they were created.

The most famous ash was the Norse World Tree, Yggdrasil, on which Odin hung, to receive the wisdom of the runes. Thus ash possesses indescribable knowledge—things we cannot really know in our heads and can only reach through expansion of consciousness. Ash fairy may bring the gift of poetry, which has the power to evoke ideas and associations that elude the conscious mind.

Ash is associated with communications of all sorts. Witches were believed to fly on ash-handled broomsticks, while Viking ships were made of ash. Many ancient cultures believed that humans originated within the ash—for instance, souls were born in the branches of Yggdrasil. The goddess Nemesis carried an ash branch. And so ash fairy teaches balance, and unity in diversity. It takes an open mind and breadth of soul to travel in the Otherworld!

Birch Fairy

This fairy is known as "the lady of the woods" for her graceful presence. Like many fairies, the birch fairy can open the portals to the subtle realms. The birch is associated with cleansing and freshness, and the goddess Arianrhod (see pages 166–168) is invoked using birch, to attract fertility and aid creativity.

Being close to the birch fairy is clearing to the mind. She will help you let go of stress and have faith in yourself, in the knowledge that you will find a way to cope. Birch is a potent female energy that brings faith and gladness. However, the birch fairy may become angry if trees near her are damaged— she holds something of the repressed energy of the feminine principle, which has been denigrated for many centuries, and she can be fierce.

If you need a clear head for a new venture, or need to leave behind you anything that is negative or contaminating, birch fairy is a great support. She will send cool, cleansing breezes that revitalize. More than any other fairy, she appreciates a little care for the Wildwood being given in return.

Beech Fairy

Like the birch, the beech fairy is a strongly feminine presence, but while birch is a "lady," beech is a queen. Sometimes known as the Mother of the Woods, she stands in stately feminine counterpart to the kingly oak. Her gifts are prosperity, but also wisdom, and she may grant wishes to those who are aware of her presence. She can help you let go of rigid ideas and move forward in faith and openness.

Beech is certainly the most graceful of the larger trees, forming beautiful woodland. And beech woods are perfect for ritual, offering shade and seclusion, but also providing clearings with space to work. The beech fairy encourages the recovery of ancient knowledge, and is especially helpful in creating a gentle, magical atmosphere.

If you feel that you are fettered by old ideas and habits and cannot see a way forward, relax in the presence of beech trees and the beech fairy will reveal a way ahead. Beech will also foster a true connection with the past, which means learning from it and retaining what is useful, without feeling confined.

Yew Fairy

The yew fairy is a venerable being indeed. She is the oldest of the tree spirits and has a depth and power that are hard to understand. Yew is an ancient evergreen, from the depths of the primeval forests that reigned across the globe before the arrival of broad-leaved trees.

Because yews are able to root their branches, they are virtually deathless, and one Scottish yew tree, the Fortingall Yew in Perthshire, is reputed to be 9,000 years old. Yews are often planted in churchyards, and are connected with death, rebirth, and initiation mysteries.

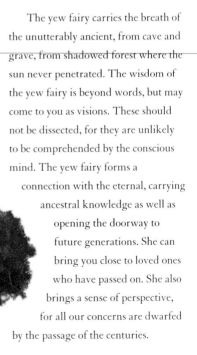

The yew fairy carries the breath of the unutterably ancient, from cave and grave, from shadowed forest where the sun never penetrated. The wisdom of the yew fairy is beyond words, but may come to you as visions. These should not be dissected, for they are unlikely to be comprehended by the conscious mind. The yew fairy forms a connection with the eternal, carrying ancestral knowledge as well as opening the doorway to future generations. She can bring you close to loved ones who have passed on. She also brings a sense of perspective, for all our concerns are dwarfed by the passage of the centuries.

Blackthorn Fairy

Blackthorn is not the gentlest of the fairy folk. It is a knobbly little tree that may be mistaken for hawthorn, but flowers earlier and often forms a hedge. Blackthorn was associated with the Dark Goddess and was considered unlucky. However, the blackthorn fairy has some very helpful gifts, for she can help us release strong emotions. This can be a cleansing experience, opening the way to new perspectives.

B lackthorn links us with our karma, highlighting barriers that can be overcome, and brings both curses and protection. The curses are the necessary negative things in life that must be dealt with in order to grow. If the blackthorn hedge that surrounded Sleeping Beauty had never imprisoned her, she would not have had her romance with the prince.

The blackthorn fairy carries the wisdom of the dark aspect of the Goddess, knowing that some things have to be destroyed if anything new is to take root. She is a crone fairy, warm and protective under her crotchety exterior. If you have been unhappy, she will help you let it all out, break through the "hedge" and find joy.

Alder Fairy

The alder tree is delicate in appearance, but is tremendously strong and is linked, as are many trees, with the creation of humans, for Irish legend tells how the first man was made from alder, and the first woman from rowan. Such stories indicate that our deepest essence is connected to that of trees—physically, karmically, and spiritually.

Alder has the gift of not decaying in water, so it is used to make bridges. Possibly because of this it is associated with the Welsh god-giant, Bran, who made his body into a bridge across the River Shannon, to invade Ireland and come to the aid of his sister, Branwen. The Welsh were victorious, but Bran was slain. His head—still living, and still possessing oracular powers—was buried in the White Hill of London, and the ravens that inhabit the Tower of London are Bran's sacred birds. It is said that England will not fall while they live there.

The alder fairy may fly forth in the form of a raven. He can impart all the secrets of good defense to you, teach you how to look for omens in bird flight and develop the gift of prophecy.

Pine Fairy

The pine fairy is an ancient spirit indeed, for pines are conifers and are among the oldest of plants, flourishing just after the glacial period and before the advent of broad-leaved trees. Scots pine is the only tree from northern Europe to have survived the Ice Age. Clumps of pine are believed to act as ley-line markers.

Pine is associated with Attis, lover of the goddess Cybele. When he was unfaithful, she changed him into a pine tree. Her son, Zeus, seeing her regret, decreed that the pine should stay green throughout the year as a consolation. Attis is one form of the dying and resurrecting god of Nature, giving pine (despite its evergreen status) a strong link with the cycles of living.

The pine fairy may be solitary and a little melancholy, but he has a healing presence and can banish negativity. The pine fairy has seen so many things come and go, and one of the things he likes to see *gone* is your lack of confidence! The wind in the pines is blowing up a new future that can help you leave your mistakes behind, for the past really is the past.

Drawing Close to Tree Fairies

The best place to approach the spirits of trees is outside, close to the trees themselves. However, there are also things you can do in your own home to bring them close.

If you can, find out what wood your furniture is made of, then research any lore and customs to do with that wood. Touch the furniture and see how it makes you feel. Try to draw close to the essence of the tree that gave its wood. This will begin to connect you with all trees of that species and their associated spirits. Give thanks for this gift of wood.

It is often possible to buy small ornaments or other artifacts made from a specific wood, and you might like to form a collection of these, in awareness of what the wood signifies. For instance, yew is often made into toadstool ornaments, as its white wood is very attractive. Yew ornaments arranged around pictures of deceased relatives honors the ancestors and the wood itself. A staff made of hazel could be used as a "talking stick" on family occasions (hazel is connected with wisdom and clear communication, so it is very appropriate for this). The idea is that the person who clutches the "talking stick" holds the floor and is listened to by everyone else. This is a Druid custom, but is adaptable to family life, for all to have their say.

If you are creative, you may like to work with wood, using a sharp knife to shape it into figures. As you do this, imagine that you are communing with the spirit of the wood and you may find that you are inspired. Twigs could be cut and bound into the shape of a five-point star. Simply making a staff with your initials or other symbols on it brings empathy with wood spirits.

We often "touch wood" for luck. This is no superstition, but a relic of a Celtic custom. In times of need a friendly tree would be approached for healing and comfort—and this is still available to us.

When buying new furniture, research the source of the wood and make sure that you only purchase from reputable, renewable resources. Wherever possible, choose second-hand furniture. Part of the function of wood is that it shall be useful, and the plant kingdom is generous with its bounty. However, it is important to be respectful and to avoid wastage wherever possible.

Drawing Close to Tree Spirits in the Wild

To tune into tree spirits in Nature, it is again important to study the lore of trees and find out what myths are associated with them, for that will help to expand your mind. However, as always, your own intuition will be your best guide, and closeness to the tree spirits will help to develop this.

Needless to say, you should spend time among trees. Make this a habit, going for walks in parks or woodland, not with the specific intention of making contact with dryads, but simply for the joy of being near trees, for their presence is very soothing. If possible camp out near them, so that you can observe them at all times of the day and sink into a dreamy sleep close to tree trunks. The spirits of many trees are more inclined to leave the tree and wander forth after nightfall, for this is a less "busy" time after the activities of the day. For this reason, people used to be afraid of being amid trees after dusk and it can be an eerie experience. However, there is nothing to fear from these beings.

Spend time getting to know one special tree. Find out as much as you can about it, its history and any stories associated with it. Touch the tree, sit leaning against it and let your mind wander. Feel yourself surrounded by the aura of the tree. How do you feel? Are you aware of beings surrounding you? Is the tree communicating with you in any way? What animals, birds, or butterflies do you see? What thoughts arise in you, and are any specific memories coming to mind? If possible, climb the tree and sit in its branches.

As you approach a special tree, try to be aware of where its aura begins. Walk slowly, with your hands held out before you, and see if you can "touch" the aura—you will feel a slight resistance, or "cushion" of air, at the point where the aura begins. Feeling the tree-aura connects you to the realm of the dryads.

Sit at a distance from the tree and let yourself fall into a dreamy state, where your eyes are slightly out of focus. What shapes or faces can you see in the foliage or bark? These are the tree spirits, making themselves known to you.

Tree-Spirit Spell for Healing

The healing benefits of trees have always been sensed by humans and, in times gone by, before we were so wedded to our logical, positivist outlook, these gifts were regularly sought by people. Many wells and springs are believed to be sacred to the Mother Goddess, and people would tie pieces of cloth to the branches of the trees surrounding such places, to draw toward them the healing gifts. These pieces of cloth were also offerings—an acknowledgment of the gifts of Nature.

METHOD

You will need a handkerchief or scarf that belongs to you. If it has specific associations—such as a handkerchief for tears cried, a bandana for migraines—so much the better. Natural fabrics are best, as these will degrade and go back to the earth. Obviously you need to be careful that you are not polluting the woodland for other users.

1 If you need healing (either physical or emotional), choose a tree that feels especially kindly. Take your handkerchief or scarf and dedicate it to healing, then place it in the branches of the tree.

2 Ask the tree spirit to take away your hurt, and leave your troubles behind in its sheltering branches.

Apple-Spirit Spell for Lasting Love

It is enjoyable to do this spell with your lover—a truly sensuous and bonding experience. However, if this isn't possible, you should tell your lover about the significance of the apple, for it is not a good idea to try and influence another person by magic, without their agreement.

METHOD

1 Sit by an apple tree in early autumn, when it is rich with fruit, and let yourself relax. Feel yourself to be a part of the tree and its bounty. Feel the presence of the apple fairy—so sweet, seductive, and bountiful.

2 Touch the bark of the apple tree and ask for all the gifts of the tree to be part of you, too. Ask to be given an apple, meant just for you and your purpose. See which fruit you feel drawn to: it may be an apple still on the tree or a "faller." As long as it is wholesome, it is right for your spell.

3 Thank the apple fairy for her gift. Cut the apple in half, crosswise, to reveal the five-point star at the center. Eat one half of the apple and give the other half to your lover, for a link that will last through time.

Meditation to Draw Close to Tree Spirits

For this meditation choose a tree with which you feel an affinity, because you see it every day or even have it in your garden. Find out about any myths connected to it, some botanical facts and what the wood is used for, to bring you close to the tree spirit.

METHOD

1 Sit with your back against the tree and ensure you will not be disturbed. If you are in a public place, have a friend keep an eye out for you and enable you to feel safe. Relax completely, as described in the Introduction (see pages 34–35), and close your eyes.

2 Imagine the aura of the tree around you. See it extending beyond the shadow cast by the tree and its branches. Feel the essence of the tree enfolding you. Be aware of rustling sounds within its branches, the breeze on your face, and any fragrance.

3 In your mind's eye, look up into the branches. Now that you are seeing with your inner sight, you are aware of many beings there. You see faces, movement, gentle eyes peeping out at you. There is a soft murmur, like the wind in the trees, but it sounds as if someone has whispered your name.

4 There is an electric sensation in your body, and you are aware of the vitality of the tree, its unique essence and magic, growing so powerfully from the earth. You are aware of its roots, penetrating into the dark, fertile soil; of the rough, warm support of the trunk; and of the exultant freedom of the branches, reaching high into the air. The aura of the tree seems to be growing stronger and the air around you is shimmering.

5 You are aware of a sensation passing through you from the tree trunk: a pleasant tingling, as if energy is moving through the tree. Beside you, a being is taking shape—slender and beautiful, surrounded by flickering green lights. This is the tree fairy. Again you hear your name being whispered gently, but more distinctly.

6 Talk to the tree fairy, asking any questions you wish. Learn the purpose of the tree, what wisdom it holds and what stories it has to tell. What message does the tree fairy have for you, and what can you do to help trees? There is a joy within trees, but there is also sadness, for so many have been sacrificed without respect. Become part of these feelings and understand their importance.

7 When your time together is over, the tree spirit will return to the tree. Bring yourself back to awareness slowly in the knowledge that your bond with the tree has been strengthened.

Meditation for the Gift of the Tree Spirits

Do this meditation to receive a healing gift from the tree spirits.
It will not necessarily be a literal gift—it could be symbolic.

METHOD

1 Begin in the same way as before (see page 366), leaning against the tree until the tree fairy emerges. Ask to be shown the wisdom of the trees and to feel the tranquillity of the dryads. Ask for any healing that you (or another person) need.

2 The tree spirit motions you to rise and moves towards the tree. Within it is a door, which swings open, revealing a shadowed entrance and a crooked stairway leading downward. You follow the spirit into the tree, marveling at the space within—truly you have entered another dimension. You descend the stairway, surrounded by a soft green glow.

3 At the bottom you find yourself in a large green chamber, with walls like tree bark and a floor of close-packed earth. At one end stands a stout lectern, supporting a heavy book. Of course books are made from trees, and for countless centuries trees have been guardians and teachers of wisdom.

4 The being opens the book. The scenes within it are living, moving ones: of primeval forests in which the trees grow thick and lush; glorious woodland; tree clusters on hilltops; floral and fruit trees; ancient and gnarled trees; solitary trees on moorland and hillside—never before have you been so aware of the aliveness of trees.

5 The scene changes and you see trees cut down and made into ships, doors

and furniture, and burnt for firewood. Still the trees are dignified and serene. Then you witness forests hacked down by machinery, wantonly destroyed by human greed. You feel guilt, hurt, and outrage, but the tree fairy puts a hand on your brow and you feel calm again. The scene in the book moves to a peaceful woodland.

6 You ask the being what you can do to help the trees. Listen for the answer: it may surprise you. Pledge to do something (even if it is only small).

7 Now it is your turn to ask for help. Explain in what way you (or a loved one) need healing. The fairy turns the pages of the great book and reaches deep within it. Within your palms is placed a special healing gift: it may be a message written on a piece of paper, a herb, a crystal, or something else.

8 Thank the tree fairy, say farewell and treasure your gift. Walk up the staircase, out into the shade of the tree. Sit down and lean against the tree trunk, letting yourself come back to everyday awareness. Do not forget your gift, or your pledge.

Weather Fairies

The Powers of the Weather Fairies

There are many fairies that influence the weather. Any of the elemental sprites—earth, fire, air, or water—may lend their energies to tempest, whirlwind, thunder, or rainstorm. The weather is an aspect of Nature over which we have no control.

Attempts to predict the weather are not always accurate, for there are complex factors involved, which can change things from minute to minute. It is said that the flutter of a butterfly's wings in one part of the world can change the weather on the other side of the globe, so subtle and delicate are the forces at work. Weather fairies are behind these forces, showing that for all our scientific achievements, there are many things that remain a mystery.

Many "good" fairies, such as Robin Goodfellow, are more active during the summer, whereas "bad" fairies appear

more in winter. This may be because the bad fairies are an embodiment of necessary decay, which is actually vital to enable new growth and is part of the natural cycle. This obviously applies to weather fairies—eternal sunshine might sound nice, but it would make life impossible!

The Story of the Snow Queen

Snow is fascinating, and to us in our centrally heated homes it is usually beautiful, and at worst a nuisance. However, not so very long ago humans were less protected from the elements, and snow could be both exquisite and terrible. The Snow Queen epitomizes forces that are part of the natural order and yet may be inimical to humans. It is tempting to demonize these energies, but they demand our respect.

The following story shows how a fascination for the Snow Queen brought out the worst in one boy, and how a girl brought him back to warmth and humanity.

A boy called Kay and a girl called Gerda had lived next door to each other since they were tiny. They were firm friends and played together always. In the summer they made daisy chains and frolicked in the wood, and in the winter they watched the snow fly from inside their warm cottages. Kay thought the snow looked like white bees, and believed there must be a

Queen Bee. One day, during a blizzard, he stood outside his door and an enormous snowflake landed on his hand. It turned into a tiny, beautiful woman, who then grew until she was taller than he was. She wore white furs, her face was pale as the moon, and her eyes were ice-blue. She smiled at him, touched his heart with a cold, cold hand, and vanished.

After this Kay was not the same. He teased Gerda, trampled on the flowers and kicked the farm animals. Spring came, and then summer, and Gerda did not recognize the boy with

whom she had once been so happy. When winter returned, Kay seemed preoccupied. He scanned the northern skies, looking for snow, and made himself a sturdy sledge. Eventually the snow came and Kay went to the market square. There he caught hold of a pearly carriage on which traveled a tall woman, wrapped in white fur, and he was never seen again.

Gerda was heartbroken. She questioned all the boys, but no one could help her. She even asked the animals and plants (for Gerda was a wise young woman, who knew the language of wild things), but even they could give her little guidance. At length she realized she would have to leave home and head for the frozen wastes of the North, if she were to have any hope of seeing Kay again. Brave Gerda went on a long and perilous journey, facing dangerous animals and murderous robbers, for her heart was full of love for Kay, even though he had been cruel to her, and she could not bear to think of him alone and cold.

Kay, of course, was in the palace of the Snow Queen, for it was she who had appeared to him in the snowflake, and who had whisked him away in the market square. He was blue with cold, and every time the Snow Queen kissed him, he went bluer. The Snow Queen's palace was made of drifting snow, hall upon empty hall stretching for miles, lit by the cold fire of the Northern Lights. Kay was making a jigsaw of lumps of

ice, which made perfect sense to him at the time. It seemed very important to get the ice to fit together, and Kay, who was clever, was determined to succeed.

The Snow Queen left her throne of ice and, telling Kay she must fly to bring snow to southern places, departed in a chilling swirl. Soon afterward Gerda found the palace and Kay inside it. With tears of joy, she ran to him and embraced him. Her tears warmed his frozen skin and melted his heart, so that he could see there was no sense to his jigsaw of ice pieces. Both the children were happier than they had ever been, and fled the Snow Queen's palace together, never to return.

WHAT THE STORY MEANS

Snow may represent the coldness of the logical mind, which seeks to control everything and put everything into a place, like the ice jigsaw, even if there is no point in this. Like the Snow Queen, this can seem a beautiful idea at first, even though it is in effect barren. The Snow Queen brings death to the heart.

And yet there is dazzling beauty in the snow. It is for humans to marvel at, but not get absorbed in. The minds and purposes of fairies are alien to mortals—small wonder that the price of entering the Snow Queen's palace may be to lose your human heart.

The Wind Knots

There are mischievous weather fairies called Folletti in Italy. These wind knots are slender, elfin creatures who love to raise storms so that they can travel on the wind. They can be cruel, rousing destructive storms that ruin the harvest, cause rivers to break their banks and blizzards to strike. They also whirl up the dust in miniature tornadoes.

S ome of the Folletti look like little boys who wear silk hats and shake castanets. They ride on whirlwinds and get into houses through cracks, where they cause all sorts of rattling noises. While many of them are well intentioned (or at least harmless), some are more sinister. For instance, the Mazzamarieddu are roused only by the blood of a murder victim and cause storms and earthquakes. Many Folletti have a strongly sexual side, and some are believed capable of raping women; the more innocuous ones take delight in blowing up the skirts of girls. Yet another species is called Grandinili and brings hail, although they can be driven off by the ringing of church bells.

Wind knots are fairies that have been demonized—but just because we do not like storms does not mean they are evil! They are vital in a scheme of things that may not prioritize humans.

Father Frost

In Russia, Father Frost embodies winter. He is a mighty spirit in a country where, when the weather is at its coldest, your out-breath may freeze as it leaves your lips, and hit the ground at your feet in a tinkling shower of tiny icicles.

Father Frost was believed to kill travelers by wrapping them in an icy embrace. Through the bare trees he would leap from branch to branch, snapping his fingers mischievously and, as he did so, every twig would be painted white with frost.

Some think of Father Frost as a smith god, because he welds together earth and water, and forges icy chains within the soil. However, in this he differs from many elf smiths, whose activities cause positive transformations. Nonetheless, there is a benevolent side to Father Frost, for like so many fairies he can be impressed by good manners. One legend tells how his cold was close to killing a girl, but she was far too polite

to say anything. Because of her restraint he spared her life.

Father Frost even has links with Father Christmas. On New Year's Day he and his daughter ride through Russia in their sleigh, laden with presents for all well-behaved children.

Thor

Thor is a mighty spirit indeed. He was a sky and thunder god of the Norse peoples, and was a favorite among farmers and sailors and all the laboring classes. Thor had a magic hammer called Mjolnir, with which he broke up the ice each summer.

Red-bearded and very strong, Thor was the son of Odin (see page 154) and Jord, the earth goddess, who was a giantess. Thor was a very important god, and Thursday is named after him. He is the Norse equivalent of Jupiter, who wielded the thunderbolts—Thor's hammer being thought of as the thunderbolt.

Thor was believed to have dominion over the air. He ruled over thunder, lightning, rain and winds, clear weather, and also fertility. Sacrifices were made to him when people were afraid of plague or famine.

Thor personifies the awesome power of Nature. He is a friend to humans, despite his strength and hot temper. If you need special encouragement to meet a challenge, call on Thor—whatever the weather, but especially when the thunder rolls. It is his message of courage.

Fog Fairies

Fairies of the fog bring images of the past and the future. While walking in the fog, it is easy to lose contact with this world. An eerie wreath of mist often surrounds barrow-mounds and stone circles. If a gap should appear in it, this forms an entrance to the Otherworld.

One particular English mist fairy is the Tiddy Mun of the fens of East Anglia. Before proper drainage, these lands were largely under water. Tiddy Mun controlled this water and any diseases it might bring, as well as the mist itself. He emerged when the mists rose at twilight, wearing a long gray gown. When the waters rose, folk would call out to Tiddy Mun to calm the water. Although he was mostly kind, Tiddy Mun could be angered. When the fens were drained, his wrath was so great that he brought illnesses to children and cows, and people had to beg his forgiveness.

When walking in the fog, note all your thoughts. The fog fairies may be giving you clues about other worlds.

Rain Fairies

Szepasszony is a beautiful Hungarian fairy, clad in a white robe, with long golden hair. She dances in rainstorms and showers of hail; she casts a spell through rainwater, dripping from the eaves to make a puddle on the ground—she then has power over anyone who steps into this puddle. Szepasszony is seductive, and not always benevolent.

She is a powerful sprite, who delights in the energies of storms. However, each rainstorm brings a host

of elemental sprites in the air within and surrounding the storm. It is a shame to shrink from contact with the rain, for raindrops can awaken your spirit and refresh your soul.

Rainbows are much associated with fairies. It is at the end of the rainbow that the Leprechaun most often hides his pot of gold. The rainbow is a bridge to the Otherworld, from where the rain fairies come. The Norse peoples called the rainbow Bifrost, and said that it was a route to Asgard, the home of the gods.

Rain not only makes the plants grow, but also brings more subtle blessings. Welcome the rain fairies, and let them wash clean your life.

Contacting the Weather Fairies

We do our best, generally, not to experience "weather," but in order to contact the electrifying energy of the weather fairies, we have to come out of our shelters. Dance in the summer rain, trace the patterns of frost, catch snowflakes, and watch the lightning play across the sky. Weather fairies bring "ordinary magic"—go to meet them!

In Nature there are few straight lines, but one situation in which they are found is when rays of sunlight slant to earth, between the clouds. A special type of fairy rides on these beams, bringing messages of hope and new perspectives. These fairies are akin to the angelic realm, and are guardians of large tracts of land. When you see these sunbeams appear, let yourself be inspired to make a wish—not just for yourself, but for the human race.

Spell to Attract a Wind Sprite

Wind sprites are the carefree gypsies of fairyland. Storm-riders,
whisperers, and mischief-makers, they bring the balm of the fragrant
breeze and the rousing blast of the tempest. They teach that all is light
and changeable, yet they also bring clarity and sharpness of mind.
You may invite wind sprites into your life, but do not think of binding
them to you—that would destroy the gifts they bring.

METHOD

You will need windchimes and some ribbon. Windchimes of bamboo will invite a gentle, thoughtful sprite who will encourage reflection. Crystal chimes will attract a highly evolved sprite to help you achieve greater detachment. Metal chimes will attract a creative sprite who can help you achieve change.

1 Choose a breezy day and hang your windchimes securely in an open window. Close your eyes and visualize the gifts you want from your sprite.

2 Lean out the window slightly so the breeze blows on your face and say:

Wind-sprite flying light and high
I call to you, draw nigh, draw nigh.
My chimes a home for you shall be
Ever welcome, ever free.

3 Listen for a special tinkle from your windchimes to tell you your sprite has arrived. Welcome this being by tying the ribbon to the upper string of the chimes, being very careful not to restrict their swaying and tinkling. Thank your sprite for being present. Whenever you feel in need of gifts from the wind sprites, stir your chimes and let a fresh breeze blow into your heart and mind.

A Dictionary of Fairies

GENERAL

Abbey lubber: A mischievous fairy that haunted abbeys, tempting monks into lustfulness and wanton living. He dwelt mostly in the wine cellar.

Black dog: This fairy appears in many places. It has supernatural powers and may be a human ghost.

Boggart: A poltergeist-type brownie.

Bogie, bogle, bug, bug-a-boo: Tormenting spirits.

Co-walker: This is the German *Doppelgänger*, a person's double; to see one is unlucky and may portend death. However, Robert Kirk (see page 18) regarded the co-walker as a fairy companion.

Fetch: The same as co-walker (see above).

Ganconer: A fairy that appears in lonely valleys, makes love to maidens and then disappears, leaving them to pine.

Goblin: A small, ugly, and malicious fairy.

Good neighbors/good people: Polite names for the fairies.

Joint-eater: A fairy who sits beside his victim and shares his food. However much the person eats, he remains thin and wan.

Mab: A diminutive fairy queen, who is probably a trivialized version of more formidable goddess figures.

Nimue: A name that is given to the Lady of the Lake.

Oberon: A name used in many stories for the Fairy King.

Seelie Court: The name given to the benign fairy host, who do such things as helping the poor and bringing good luck.

Titania: The Fairy Queen in Shakespeare's *A Midsummer Night's Dream*. This was not a name that was often used for the Fairy Queen, and is a variant of Diana.

Young Tam Lin or Tamlane: A young knight kidnapped by the Fairy Queen and brought back to the human world through the bravery of fair Janet, who loved him and held him fast through some terrifying fairy shape-shifting.

AUSTRALIAN

Alcheringa: Fairies known to the Arunta tribes of central Australia—thin, wraithlike, but youthful. They must be placated, but sometimes act as guardian spirits.

BELGIAN

Kludde: A shape-shifting Belgian fairy who attacks at dawn and sunset. It may appear as a black cat, black dog, or snake.

CELTIC/IRISH

Angus mac Og: A Celtic god of youth and beauty, one of the Tuatha de Danann, who were defeated by the Milesians and became the people of the Sidhe, who inhabit barrow mounds. Angus was son of the Dagda, the "Good God," and lived in Brug na Boinne.

Bean Sidhe ("banshee"): An Irish death-spirit who wails when a true Irish person is about to die. Her eyes are fiery red from weeping, her hair streams and she dresses in gray and green.

Cailleach Bera: A gigantic Irish hag fairy.

Cuchulain: A mythological Ulster hero, son of Lugh, god of light, of the Tuatha de Danann. His strength was tremendous, but he was also skilled in magic, poetry, and music.

Dagda: The High King of the Tuatha de Danann, the immortal Irish fairy folk. He had four magnificent palaces within the Hollow Hills.

Dana/Danu: A great Irish mother goddess, ancestor of the Tuatha de Danann.

Daoine Sidhe: Another name for the Tuatha de Danann.

Etain: A heroine of the fairy romance with Midhir, of the Tuatha de Danann. This story is retold in the play *The Immortal Hour* by Fiona MacCleod.

Fin Bheara ("fin-vara"): The Fairy King of Ulster, also sometimes regarded as the king of the dead. He rides a black horse and resides in his fairy mound of Knockma.

Fion mac Cumhail ("fin ma-cool"): A hero descended from the Tuatha de Danann, about whom there are many tales. Leader of the mighty Fianna, a famous band of warriors.

Firbolgs: The first inhabitants of Ireland, giant and grotesque, conquered by the Tuatha de Danann.

Fomorians: Demons who fought against the Irish fairy races. They were finally defeated by the Tuatha de Danann at Moytura.

Lugh: One of the Tuatha de Danann, the god of brightness, patron of crafts and all manner of skills. Son of the Dagda (see left), he killed Balor, leader of the Fomorians, and put an end to the long war.

Macha: One of the forms of the Irish war goddess, a fairy that revels amongst the slain.

Manannan mac Lir: Chief Irish god of the sea, protector of the Isle of Man and owner of magic swine that fed the Tuatha de Danann.

Morrigan: One of the forms of the Irish war goddess, who gave Cuchulain (see left) his stupendous strength.

Oonagh: One of the wives of Fin Bheara, robed in silver gossamer, with golden hair that sweeps the ground.

Phooka: An Irish bogey-beast, often appearing as an ugly horse.

Tom Cockle: An Irish fairy who had served one family for generations. When the family fell into poverty and had to leave Ireland, they bid a sorrowful goodbye to Tom Cockle; but when they crossed the seas and came to their new house, they found a fire already burning and food laid out, for Tom Cockle had come with them.

CENTRAL EUROPEAN (ITALIAN/AUSTRIAN/SWISS)

Aguana: A shape-shifting female fairy from Italy and Austria, beautiful and with a lovely voice, but goat's feet. She guards streams and may drown those who harm her.

Erdluittle: This name means "Earth Folk." This fairy comes from Switzerland and northern Italy and brings fertility, but may steal human babies. It is very dark, with duck's feet.

CHINESE

Hu Hsien: Malicious Chinese fox fairies, who are able to change their shape. Hsian is a term for an immortal spirit.

ENGLISH

Apple-tree man: A Somerset fairy who dwells in the oldest apple tree in the orchard.

Asrai: A delicate water fairy from Shropshire, who melts away when captured.

Black Annis: A hag fairy from Leicestershire, probably a demonized crone-goddess.

Brag: A mischievous goblin from the northern counties of England, who often changes into a horse.

Brown man of the muirs: A Border Counties guardian spirit of wild beasts.

Bucca: A Cornish spirit, who is given bread and beer for luck.

Colt-pixy: A sprite that takes the form of a horse. In Hampshire this fairy plays havoc with real horses, but in Somerset (in the form of a pony) it guards orchards.

Derrick: A dwarf-like fairy of Devon, who is rather malevolent.

Dobby: A mischievous Yorkshire and Lancashire hobgoblin—obviously an inspiration for Dobby in the *Harry Potter* stories!

Fenoderee/Phynnodderee: A Manx Brownie, who is large, ugly, and hairy. Some say he was once a graceful fairy, but he fell in love with a mortal girl and left the autumn festival to dance with her. For this he was banished from Fairyland.

Grindylow: A Yorkshire water demon, who lurks in stagnant pools to drown children.

Padfoot: A bogey-beast from the countryside around Leeds, sometimes appearing as a white dog. Padfoot is the alter ego of Sirius, Harry's godfather in the *Harry Potter* books.

Skillywidden: A little fairy caught by a farmer at Treridge, in Cornwall. He was only 1 ft. (30 cm) high and was found asleep on the heath. He played with the children until his parents came for him.

Spriggan: An ugly West Country fairy who acts as a bodyguard to others of his kind, inhabiting ruins where treasure is buried.

Tryamour: Daughter of the Fairy King Olyroun, she married one of King Arthur's knights, Sir Launfal. Not only was she wondrously beautiful, but Tryamour also brought great riches—all on condition that Sir Launfal did not disclose their union. When insulted by Guinevere, Launfal made the mistake of boasting about his love, and for this he was punished by Tryamour's disappearance, with all her gifts. Launfal was due to be banished, when his fairy love rode up, to prove that she was more beautiful than Guinevere and take him away to Fairyland.

Yallery Brown: An evil fairy from the Fens, found crying beneath a stone by a laborer called Tom Tiver. Initially Yallery Brown did Tom's work for him, but because he wrecked the work of others, Tom became unpopular. He thanked the fairy sarcastically, whereupon he had ill luck to the end of his days.

FRENCH

Abundia: Dark-haired queen of the Normandy fairies, who wears a circlet with a star on her forehead.

Dames vertes: Eastern French fairies who live in forests and caves, near waterfalls and springs. They are stately, beautiful, and clad in green. Although they bless the crops and sometimes help in the house, they can be very dangerous, especially to men who love them.

GERMAN

Alp: A German fairy that causes nightmares by sitting on the sleeper's chest.

Berchte (The Bright One): A German fairy with many characteristics: she may be a hag or a bringer of presents at Epiphany.

HAWAIIAN

Menahune: Hawaiian fairies who have little bows and arrows that they shoot, to pierce the hearts of the angry and make them love instead. They may act as house fairies, especially to those who have menahune blood.

INDIAN

Indra: Supreme god of the Hindu pantheon, later demoted to the status of King of the Fairies. He is very amorous and lives in Koh Qaf, the land of the fairies.

INUIT

Nuliarksak: An Inuit fairy lover, who may marry a human and have his children, but they will be invisible.

JEWISH

Mazikeen: Shape-shifting Jewish fairies who can foretell the future and perform magic. Occasionally they may marry humans.

MAORI

Patu-paiarehe: Maori fairies whose songs may be heard, even though they are invisible. They live in bushes in the forks of trees, where the fairy flax grows. They may play tricks on humans, and red fruit is sacred to them.

NATIVE AMERICAN

Kachinas: Nature spirits of the Hopi and Pueblo Native Americans. They include the Cloud Beings, Star Spirits, Corn Maidens, Dawn Spirits, and Lightning Spirits. Human dead may become cloud spirits. Kachinas teach humans many skills. They are present from midwinter to midsummer, and for the following six months they return to the Otherworld. They always come when summoned, and are invoked by mask-wearing Kachina dancers.

Manitou: Native American horned nature spirits that play tricks on humans. "Manitou" is also the generic term for life-force, or "chi."

Sasquatch: The North American Bigfoot, 6½-10 ft. (2–3 m) tall and covered in hair. There are reports of similar creatures from all around the world.

PERSIAN

Peries: Persian good fairies, made from fire. They may take the shape of doves, leaving their plumage by the water's edge to bathe as humans. A human man who steals their garments may marry a Peri, in similar fashion to the Selkie (see page 106), with similar tragic results.

POLYNESIAN

Atua: Polynesian fairies who inhabit trees and fly, but may help around the house and marry humans. They are nature spirits and highly honored.

RUSSIAN

Baba Yaga: A Russian hag fairy who lives in a magic house that walks on chicken legs. She rewards the good, but eats those who displease her.

Bannik: A domestic fairy of the Russian bath-house, sometimes glimpsed in the steam. If well treated, he brings luck. Offerings of tree branches and soap are made to him.

Leshy: A tree fairy, often found near fly agaric mushrooms. This Russian forest guardian may be tricky.

Rusalki: Russian wood nymphs or water fairies. They bring fertility and have power over the weather. They may be a remnant of ancient goddess worship, and are very powerful and sometimes dangerous.

SCANDINAVIAN

Aelf: A Scandinavian form of "elf," a nature spirit who sometimes brings sickness.

Ellefolk: Danish nature fairies who possess ancient knowledge and the power to foretell the future. The females are beautiful, but they have hollow backs and cow's tails and like to seduce young men. The males are old and may bring pestilence.

SCOTTISH

Bean-nighe: The Scottish equivalent of the Banshee.

Blue men of the Minch: These fairies haunted the strait between Long Island and Shiant Islands and caused shipwrecks.

Cailleach Bheur: The Scottish version of Cailleach Bera (see page 387), who is associated with winter and wild beasts (in Ulster called Cally Berry).

Ceasg: A Highland mermaid who may grant three wishes if caught. Sometimes she may be prevailed upon to marry a human, in a similar way to the Selkie (see page 106).

Crodhe Mara: Highland fairy sea-cattle, which may lead real cattle into a fairy mound, so that they disappear for ever. However, if a sea-bull mates with an ordinary cow, the herd stock is greatly improved.

Each Uisge ("ech-ooshkya"): A Highland water horse of the most evil kind, haunting lochs and the sea.

Fachan: A very ugly Highland fairy, with one hand, one leg, and one eye.

Habetrot: A Borderlands fairy who is the patron of spinning.

People of Peace: The Highland equivalent of the Daoine Sidhe of Ireland (see page 387), but without their hierarchy. They are trooping fairies that live in the Hollow Hills. "People of Peace" or "People of the Hills" may also be a general euphemism for fairies, to keep them happy!

Redcap: A malignant Border Counties goblin, who lived in ruined castles where evil had been done and dyed his cap in human blood.

Silky: A female fairy from the Borders, who wears rustling silk as she does the household jobs and terrorizes lazy servants.

Sluagh: The Scottish host of the Unforgiven Dead—usually perceived in the air, around midnight, and considered the most sinister of the fairy folk.

Unseelie Court: These are malevolent Scottish fairies, including the Sluagh, Redcaps and many solitary fairies.

SPANISH

Duendes: Spanish house fairies who look like middle-aged women, with long fingers. They come out at night to clean and repair, and can be malicious to anyone who causes a mess.

TURKISH

Cin: Shape-shifting Turkish fairies— usually invisible, sometimes friendly, but sometimes malevolent. They may appear as animals, humans, or giants, and are ruled by a king.

WELSH

Gwyllion: Evil Welsh mountain fairies, ugly women who mislead travelers by night.

Morgan: A water spirit. Morgan le Fay was King Arthur's evil fairy, although she was one of the fairies that carried him to Avalon.

Plant Annwn: Welsh fairies that dwell in the Underworld. The entrance to their realm is via lakes. Gwyn Ap Nudd is their king.

Plant Rhys Dwfen: This means "Family of Rhys the Deep" and is the name for a fairy tribe that inhabits an invisible land (invisible because of an indigenous herb). These fairies came to the market in Cardigan and paid high prices.

Select Bibliography

A Dictionary of Fairies, Katherine Briggs, Penguin, 1977.

Enchantment of the Faerie Realm, Ted Andrews, Llewellyn, 2005.

The Faerie Way, Hugh Mynne, Llewellyn, 1998.

The Faeries Oracle, Brian Froud and Jessica Macbeth, Simon & Schuster, 2000.

Fairy Magic, Rosemary Ellen Guiley, Element, 2004.

The Secret Lives of Elves & Fairies, from the Private Journal of the Rev. Robert Kirk, John Matthews, Godsfield, 2005.

Index

Acknowledgments

Executive Editor Sandra Rigby

Editor Charlotte Macey

Executive Art Editor Sally Bond

Designer Annika Skoog for Cobalt ID

Illustrators Nick Harris, Jon Goode, James Holderness, Dean Spencer

Senior Production Controller Simone Nauerth

Picture Researcher Giulia Hetherington

PICTURE CREDITS